GAOUSSOU MARICO

Ethics and performance

Symbiosis as a significant basis for the development of industrial companies

ScienciaScripts

Imprint

Cover image: www.ingimage.com

This book is a translation from the original published under ISBN 978-620-6-70109-5.

Publisher:
Sciencia Scripts
is a trademark of
Dodo Books Indian Ocean Ltd. and OmniScriptum S.R.L publishing group

120 High Road, East Finchley, London, N2 9ED, United Kingdom
Str. Armeneasca 28/1, office 1, Chisinau MD-2012, Republic of Moldova, Europe

ISBN: 978-620-7-30340-3

Table of contents

DEDICATION

I dedicate this book

In memory of my parents, the late Barasson MARICO and the late Awa DEMBELE. I pray to God, the Almighty, that He welcomes them into the Holy Paradise.

INTRODUCTION

Ethics and performance are two polysemous concepts. Their meanings vary in time and space.

Etymologically, ethics comes from the Greek "ethos", which was a term used to designate a way of behaving that conformed to the established moral order. In its contemporary sense, ethics refers to morals, the conduct of life and the rules of behavior established by a given social body. Philosophically speaking, ethics is the science of morality. It refers to all the moral conceptions of an individual or a social milieu. In politics, it is the fundamental reflection carried out by the people to establish their standards, limits and duties. In management, ethics refers to the attitude or behavior of a person, a group of people or a structured organization. When applied to companies, it covers both the individual behavior of employees and the behavior of the legal entity, both in its strategy and in its day-to-day conduct of business.

In the context of our present work, we see ethics as the attitude of companies to integrate the expectations of different stakeholders into their economic choices, through the implementation of the following decision-making principles: respect for employees, expressed in particular through the establishment of proper working conditions; providing shareholders, customers and suppliers with information on their products; taking into account the effects of business activity on the environment; participation in the social life of the community (patronage, sponsorship, foundations); and constant respect for human rights in all their dimensions.

As for the term performance, it is thought to derive from English performance, coming either from Middle English to perform - to which the suffix of French origin (ance) would have been added - or from Old French parformer or Middle French parformance (attested around 1571-72)[1] . From its first appearance to the present day, the meaning of this word has not changed fundamentally. Today, as in the 16th century, the word performance refers to "the ability of a person or entity to perform an action, or to the magnitude of the result of an action, with reference to an objective and an expected outcome" (Notat 2007). In business terms, this means assessing the level of achievement of results in relation to the efforts made and resources consumed. It follows from this meaning that the notion of performance goes hand in hand with the related notions of effectiveness and efficiency, whose combined evaluation forms the

---

[1] Dictionnaire de l'Académie française, eighth edition, 1932-1935

barometer capable of providing an objective measure of a company's performance (Bourguignon 1997).

For the purposes of the present work, we will understand performance as being the company's ability to achieve its raison d'être, i.e. to make profits while limiting the resources to be consumed or the capital to be committed.

In the fourth millennium BC, the relationship between ethics and performance corresponded to the interrelation between morality - synonymous with ethics - and economics. Ancient Greek philosophers and medieval theologians always considered economics and morality to be inseparable. In this sense, Plato believed that economics - as the practical art of ensuring the sustenance of the city - was an activity reserved for rulers. Because these rulers were also the holders of political power, and because this power was to be entrusted only to the most virtuous men, i.e. those capable of acting wisely[2], economics in Platonic thought is a set of activities that cannot properly exist without being circumscribed by ethics[3]. In the 16th century, this superimposed logic gradually faded with the emergence of mercantilism.

For mercantilists, the power of a state depends on its ability to generate substantial trade between itself and its neighbors. According to them, the economy had only one objective: the pursuit of profit, and for this reason, economic agents could not allow themselves to be constrained by moral or religious considerations when interacting on the markets[4]. Thanks to these presuppositions, mercantilists succeeded in gaining public acceptance for colonization and the unorthodox exploitation mechanisms used by European transnational companies to exploit, among other things, the people and raw materials of the New World.

In the era of the Industrial Revolution, the rise of liberal thinking exacerbated the split between ethics and morality begun by the mercantilists. Indeed, classical economists such as Adam Smith[5] believed that the market economy required economic agents to dispense with all moral considerations, since ethics, as a means of regulating the economy, was not necessary in a market economy. This type of economy would be self-regulating, since according to Smith,

---

[2] For Socrates, in line with Plato, wisdom is the cardinal notion of virtue. From it flow four cardinal qualities whose combined presence confers virtuous status on those who possess them. These qualities are: courage, temperance, justice and piety.

[3] Marc Antoine GAVRAY, la définition platonicienne de la vertu, Annuaire de l'EPHE, section des Sciences religieuses (2010-2011), pp. 103-110

[4] In the economic sense

[5] Adam Smith, Scottish moral philosopher and economist *born 1766, died 1834*

the satisfaction of the general interest - the main contribution of the combination of ethics and morality - would, in market economies, spring from the sum of the selfish pursuit of personal satisfaction by the economic agents active there. Philosopher André Comte-Sponville has recently taken this line of reasoning, which has come to be known as the "invisible hand" mechanism, to new extremes. In his book entitled "Is capitalism moral?", Sponville summed up this thesis rather cynically, asserting that "just as there are no morals in arithmetic, no morals in physics, no morals in meteorology" (...) there would be none "in economics!" Thus, at the dawn of the 20th century, economics had become the symbol of the individualistic, every-man-for-himself sentiment that was spreading through Western societies[6].

At present, the trend seems to be reversing. Over the past few decades, we have observed that, as a result of repeated scandals, recurring crises and the significant impact of business on society and the environment, economic theories are becoming increasingly permeated by ethical considerations. As a matter of fact, according to the Nobel Prize-winning economist Amartya Sen[7], economics today is a science with two origins, both linked in different ways to politics: one, based on "mechanics" (a term to be understood here in the mathematical sense of rational mechanics) and devoted primarily to logistical problems, while the other, concerned with ultimate ends and the "human good", is based on ethical reflection and linked to a moral vision of politics. In essence, the economy as an autonomous subject is presented in this book not as the tautological goal of any society, but rather as a tool predestined to serve, to make a society more just, more humane. With this approach, the author puts his finger on the inseparability of ethics and economics in today's capitalist world[8].

According to a Marxist-inspired definition, capitalism is characterized first and foremost by the pursuit of profit, the accumulation of capital and wage-earning[9]. In pre-capitalist

---

[6] From Mauriac, Renaud Chazal. "Au fil du temps.... Justice des mineurs", *Les Cahiers Dynamiques*, vol. 37, no. 1, 2006, pp. 82-86.

[7] Amartya Sen, born in 1933, Indian economist and humanist, Nobel Prize winner in economics in 1998

[8] Capitalism really took off with the fall of the Berlin Wall in 1989. The reunification of the two blocs symbolized by this fall is considered by the doctrine to be the sign of the decline of Socialism and Communism, the economic currents that had prevailed until then. Capitalism is opposed to communism, which aims to put an end to the exploitation of the proletariat - a class made up of those who do not live adequately from the fruits of their labor - through the collective appropriation of all means of production and exchange, with the aim of establishing a classless society. It is similar to socialism, in that both advocate corporate ownership. Their difference lies in the identity of the holder of this property right. For socialists, this right belongs to the state, in which case we speak of nationalization, whereas for communists, this right belongs to the collective, to the community. In capitalism, property rights are granted only to private individuals or companies, hence the term "privatization". In short, socialism is a kind of state monopoly, or rather, state capitalism.

[9] Wage-earning is a production system in which workers do not own their tools, but rather their labor power.

systems, the craftsman owned his tools. In the capitalist system, the contributor of capital not only owns the tools of production, but also the company as a whole. This creates a disparity in the distribution of the wealth created. The owner of the capital, although not the one who directly produces the goods and services offered by the company, will be the one who derives the maximum benefit. It was undoubtedly this state of affairs that prompted Karl Marx to say[10] that capitalism was "the exploitation of man by man". However, this statement, which implies that there are no ethics in the capitalist economy, was refuted by Max Weber[11].

For Weber, the disparity in the distribution of wealth that distinguishes capitalism is an entirely ethical reality, insofar as it is the logical result of the advent of the "spirit of capitalism"; a spirit that presupposes that individuals living in capitalist societies have an ethic of their own, a capitalist ethic as it were. According to this approach, the unbridled pursuit of profit is the profound nature of capitalist man, erected in capitalist society as the archetype of the man to whom everyone should aspire. Consequently, in capitalist societies, the entrepreneur is the central figure of society, the most ethical of all men, because by making investment his priesthood, he embodies the soul of society, the "spirit of capitalism". He gives up his personal comfort to invest in companies designed to create wealth and progress. He also provides jobs for other members of society.

The direct consequence of this Weberian approach to capitalism is that, in capitalist societies, the enterprise - in the sense of a trading company[12] - is an inescapable entity, as it has an impact on society as a whole. The effects of its activities are no longer felt solely by the investors and employees who have enabled it to come into being and prosper. They are felt by all the components of the social body established in the geographical area in which it is based, or in the zones where its main activities are located. Japanese culture is rooted in the Weberian foundations of capitalism. On the strength of this culture, the specific features of the Japanese company are attributable in particular to the collective will to succeed and the organizational rigor of work (effort, devotion, commitment, involvement). Indeed, the Japanese company functions as a community (collective values). The organization and its members have a long-term vision of the company, and work on the basis of trust and loyalty[13].

---

[10] Karl Heinrich Marx, born May 5, 1818 in Trier, Rhineland, and died March 14, 1883 in London, was a German historian, journalist, philosopher, economist and sociologist.
[11] Max Weber, born on April 21, 1864 and died on June 14, 1920, was a German economist and sociologist.
[12] Legally distinct from non-trading companies.
[13] Carole Doueiry Verne and Olivier Meier, Culture and ethics, A look at Japan and Japanese companies

And yet, despite its vital role, until the second half of the 20th century, few studies by capitalist authors focused specifically on the company. At the time, the firm was regarded simply as a "black box". For classical and neoclassical economists, the function of the firm boiled down to a simple objective: to be a structure capable of maximizing, in a competitive environment, the profit of the entrepreneur who, as well as being its creator, was also its manager. It wasn't until the 1930s, with changes in market structure and strong concentration movements, that a new literature on the notion of the company appeared. This included Berle and Means' 1932 work, evocatively entitled "The Modern Corporation and Private Property". In this work, these authors sketched out a redefinition of the concept of firm or enterprise in the light of "agency theory". According to this theory, the firm is the center of reconciliation of at least two, a priori, dissonant interests. Indeed, drawing on the consequences of the "metamorphosis" of companies with the generalization of joint-stock companies[14] , the authors presented the company no longer as the place where two dissonant interests cooperate, but rather as the meeting place for a multitude of specific interests carried by people - natural or legal - referred to as "stakeholders"[15] .

Initially, the aforementioned multitude corresponded only to a quadripartite interaction between shareholders, managers, employees and customers, made possible by the elevation of managers to stakeholder status in response to the need to deal with the operational risks posed by the over-concentration of owners omnipresent in the majority of joint-stock companies. Indeed, when an organization is faced with a situation that requires it to take decisive action, a plethora of decision-makers makes it virtually impossible to reach a consensus, and this is precisely what happens in most joint-stock companies. Given that operational decision-making in companies is a time when slowness does not go down well, a mechanism had to be put in place to ensure that, during these critical times when speed is of the essence, the decision-

[14] E. Penrose, "Strategy/ Organization and the Metamorphosis of the Large Firm", 1994, reprinted in *Organization Studies*, vol. 29, 2008, pp. 1117-1024.

[15] In pre-capitalist companies, the enterprise was the convergence of a single antagonism whose stakeholders were shareholders and employees. According to this conception, on one side were the shareholders - owners of the means of production - and on the other were the employees, holders of the workforce. And in this relationship, the former would seek only to make their capital profitable, while the latter would be in search of rewards - such as wages - that would compensate for the indentation of their labour power to the shareholders' ambition of employing them to produce goods and services destined to be marketed. As a result, the opposition between shareholders and employees was based on the fact that the compensation demanded by the latter required: if we place ourselves upstream of sales, that the capital invested by the former be used up even before the products it was intended to produce had been developed or sold; and if we place ourselves downstream of sales, that the sales generated once the products had been marketed be heavily deducted by payroll costs.

making process is not hampered by the cacophony caused by the presence of a plethora of decision-makers. The solution adopted by most legal bodies governing the creation of joint-stock companies has been to oblige shareholders to transfer to managers the usus they have over the shares they own. As a result, the power of control shifted from the owners of the capital to the managers. Now, in the majority of joint-stock companies worldwide, the responsibility for making operational decisions lies with managers. More specifically, the role of these agents - who, in companies, are generally equidistant between the status of employee and shareholder - is to take operational decisions capable of reducing the "transaction costs"[16] in order to enhance the company's performance.

For Berle and Means, this shift in power corresponds to the separation of "control and management" functions, with management belonging to managers and control to shareholders. This separation, because of the asymmetrical dyarchy it creates at the head of companies, can, if not properly supervised, lead to the cohabitation of irreconcilable interests - on the one hand, those of managers and, on the other, those of owners[17] - where the aim should be the harmonious interrelation of distinct interests. This risk of misappropriation, inherent in the perception of the company in terms of agency theory, was undoubtedly the trigger for the development of a whole body of law dedicated to the criminal and civil repression of damage caused to companies by managers[18].

In the second half of the twentieth century, financial literature focused on mechanisms to prevent the risk of misappropriation of power induced by the emergence of managerial ownership (Jensen and Meckling, 1976; Agrawal and Mandelker, 1990; Brickley, Lease and Smith, 1988; Fama and Jensen, 1983; Mehran, 1995; Jensen and Ruback, 1983; Fama, 1980; Hart, 1983). Authors belonging to the "shareholder approach" believed that shareholder satisfaction was the ultimate reason for the company's existence.

This shareholder approach was already illustrated by the Dodge brothers' 1919 lawsuit against Ford Motors. In this high-profile case, the Michigan Supreme Court ruled in favor of the Dodge brothers, who, as minority shareholders in Ford Motors, demanded that the company

---

[16] The paternity of this "transaction cost" theory is attributed to Oliver Williamson, who expressed it perfectly in his book: The Economic Institutions of Capitalism, Free Press, 1985. The French translation was published in 1994 by éditions interédition under the title: Les institutions de l'économie.
[17] Ould Daoud Ellili, Nejla. "Managerial ownership, board characteristics and shareholder wealth", *La Revue des Sciences de Gestion*, vol. 224-225, no. 2-3, 2007, pp. 143-154.
[18] The omnipresence in the majority of legal systems of legal actions that are very similar to the Ut Singuli action in French law is ample proof of the topicality of this concern.

distribute its surplus profits in the form of dividends (see Blair, 1995, p. 51), instead of using them for employee stock grants. Indeed, in 1916, Ford Motors had made very substantial profits. Henry Ford, as majority shareholder (58% of the shares), decided not to distribute everything in the form of dividends, and to use the surplus profits to finance a social policy consisting of lowering the selling price of vehicles, while maintaining their level of quality, and hiring more people. The avowed aim was that the company's employees should also be able to afford the vehicles they produced. Minority shareholders John and Horace Dodge (10% of the shares) vigorously contested this decision and demanded higher dividends. Having failed to find an amicable solution to their dispute with Ford, the two brothers took the case to the Michigan Court, which was called upon to decide the following question: was it possible for a company's principal shareholder - and therefore its main strategic decision-maker - to manage the company for charitable rather than purely economic purposes?

After hearing the arguments of the parties, particularly those of Ford, who defended itself with ardor and obstinacy, the verdict pronounced by the Court was unequivocal. Basing itself on the principle that "the shareholders are the sole owners of the company", the Court affirmed that "the company (must) first be organized for the profit of its shareholders" and that, as a result, "the discretionary latitude of the directors (could) only be mobilized for this purpose and that, in no case, (this discretionary latitude could) lead to the reduction of profits or to their non-distribution for the benefit of the community (...)".

The Ford vs Dodge decision symbolizes the intensification in the 20th century of the opposition between economics and ethics. It is said to be a manifestation of the ethical egoism of capitalism, advanced by Weber before being systematized by the ultra-liberal Milton Friedman[19]. For him, a company's only social responsibility is to increase its profits.

It's worth noting that, despite the court's verdict, Ford persisted in its plan to pay workers higher wages in order to increase their purchasing power and turn them into potential future customers. This vision of business, which today would be described as ethical, spread around the world under the name "Fordist compromise". And it seems that the longevity of Ford, one of the world's largest automakers one hundred years after its creation, owes much to its implementation.

---

[19] Milton Friedman (1912-2006), American economist, winner of the 1976 Nobel Prize in Economics, considered by his peers to be an ultraliberal thinker because of his propensity to support theses such as "a company's only social responsibility is to increase its profit".

In the mid-1970s, having restored capitalism to its former glory in liberal societies, the Fordist compromise began to lose its lustre. A series of oil shocks triggered an economic recession that finally sounded the death knell of the thirty glorious years[20] .

In the early 80s, following the oil crisis, economic activity picked up again, driven by growing demand for manufactured goods. To keep pace with these developments, industrial companies had to grow in size and complexity. The resulting omnipresence of transactions in all aspects of social life made the company the producer of externalities - in the economic sense of the term - both negative and positive on the entire social environment around it. As a result, it had become untenable to consider this organization as solely the business of shareholders and managers. Companies were now the business of society as a whole. This "deprivatization" led to an extension of the scope of the term "stakeholder" from just shareholders, managers and employees to include "any group or individual who may affect or be affected by the achievement of the company's objectives" Freeman (1984).

Thus, we moved from a reductionist approach - the shareholder approach - to an extensive approach - the partnership approach - which sees the company as a nexus of contracts bringing together different stakeholders. Henceforth, the company was to be considered as the center for reconciling at least five specific interests: 1) the interest of shareholders - to make the capital invested profitable - 2) the interest of managers - to maintain an enviable position in a world where social success is often synonymous with the financial success their positions are likely to bring them - 3) the interest of employees - to benefit from rewarding working conditions in return for their participation in the enrichment of shareholders - 4) the interest of the company as a legal entity - to be competitive in order to continue to exist - 5) and finally, the interests of customers, who, in the early days of this theory, were seen only as economic agents whose main concern was to satisfy their consumption needs. To these must be added the state and the community as a whole, which expects a healthy environment and tax and social benefits.

---

[20] This is a chrononym used to designate the three decades of strong growth and rising living standards experienced by the majority of developed countries between 1945 (after the Second World War) and 1975.

Thanks to this new approach to the role of the company, the question of ethics was reaffirmed as the central notion of the corporate concept. Ethics were no longer confined to the implementation of "paternalistic management[21] ", but penetrated the very being of companies, with the emergence of resolutely ethical social forms[22] .

In 1987, the emergence of the concept of sustainable development from the pen of Norwegian Prime Minister Gro Harlem Brundland accelerated this movement to moralize capitalism. Sustainable development is a form of development that meets the needs of present generations without compromising the ability of future generations to meet their own needs. The legalization of this new type of development has forced companies to take account of non-economic objectives in their operations. In recent years, we have witnessed the rise of a growing number of movements calling for a reform of capitalism. In industrialized countries, these voices are winning decisive victories for the legal devolution of a greater social role to companies. In France, the PACTE Act (Plan d'Action pour la Croissance et la Transformation des Entreprises) adopted in May 2019 is a telling example of this shift in approach. Indeed, this law introduced into French law the status of mission company, which obliges companies to assign themselves, through their bylaws, several social and environmental objectives that they will make it their mission to pursue in the course of their business. This obligation is fully in line with the requirement now imposed on French companies to include consideration of the social and environmental issues inherent in their activity in their decision-making processes[23] . In this respect, the PACTE Act should be seen as bringing French law into line with legislation in other industrialized countries. Indeed, for several years now, similar provisions have existed in the legislation of several Anglo-Saxon countries, such as the United States, which have traditionally taken a purely shareholder-based approach to business.

The popularization of ethics in business has been driven by a number of socio-political and economic events and situations.

At international level, the first major initiative was proposed on January 31, 1999, at the World Economic Forum in Davos. During this forum, the then UN Secretary General, Mr. Kofi Annan, proposed a Global Compact, aimed at forging a voluntary partnership between the UN,

---

[21] Michelle Perrot, "Le regard de l'Autre: les patrons français vus par les ouvriers (1880-1914)", Cahiers du Mouvement social, no 4, 1979, pp. 293-306.
[22] Corporate citizenship, ethical funds and socially responsible investment.
[23] Art. 1833 of the French Civil Code.

11

business, governments and civil society to promote dialogue and exchange on good corporate practice in the areas of human rights, labor law, environmental protection and anti-corruption.

At national level, the moralization of capitalism has been driven by two factors: one external or exogenous, the other internal or endogenous. The external factor that has accelerated the penetration of the ethical approach to business is due to international community organizations (UN, EU, ECOWAS, UEMOA, AU, etc.) which, in the early 2000s, began to develop and monitor the implementation by States and their private sectors of binding legal frameworks relating to environmental protection, the fight against money laundering and the financing of terrorism[24].

Complementing this exogenous pressure was an endogenous push from national trade unions, which at the same time began to demand more active employee participation in corporate decision-making[25]. This union vigor, because of the advances it enabled, can be seen as the catalyst for the deployment, in the private sector, of the concept of corporate social responsibility (CSR)[26]; a concept which, as we shall see in greater depth, is the anchor for the notion of ethics in many Malian or foreign companies operating in Mali[27].

In addition, with the advent of decentralization and higher levels of education, communities - and therefore customers and prospects - are increasingly seeking to understand the impact of companies on society, whether in terms of employment, tax payments, environmental impact, pollution or resource depletion. This heightened awareness of sustainable development issues has led many consumers to adopt Socially Responsible Consumption (SRC).

This new type of consumption, which by the way is quite recent[28], generally manifests itself in an economic agent taking "into account, prior to any act of purchase, the public consequences" of the envisaged purchase in order to be able to use "his purchasing power to induce (often positive) changes in society" (Webster, 1975).

---

[24] Alexandre Wong and Urbain Kiswend-Sida Yaméogo, Les responsabilités sociétales des entreprises en Afrique francophone, Le livre blanc, ed. Charles Léopold Mayer, 2011, pp. 26 - 37.
[25] Guide syndical orientation et information, Friedrich Eibert Foundation, December 2016, p. 64.
[26] The revaluation of the SMIG since January 1er 2016 in Mali is a fabulous testimony to the ability of trade unions to drive positive social change. Indeed, this increase is the direct consequence of the mobilization of workers' unions against the dehumanizing wage practices of certain employers.
[27] See the draft Corporate Social Responsibility Policy of the Banque de Développement du Mali - SA, available on the Internet at the following link: Politique-RSE.pdf (bdm-sa.com)
[28] François-Lecompte, Agnès. "La consommation socialement responsable : oui mais...", Reflets et perspectives de la vie économique, vol. xlviii, no. 4, 2009, pp. 89-98.

It seems that in an urban context, the CRS is less well-established than in a rural one. In cities, excessive urbanization and its eternal corollary: the rising cost of living, mean that the price of goods or services is often a major factor in triggering the act of purchase. In many cases, the prospect of the potential extra costs that CRS is likely to entail is enough to atrophy the desire to consume ethically. Recent research into the development of CRS, however, suggests a trend towards a lessening of the impact of the price factor on people's willingness to consume ethically. In the space of a decade, thanks to awareness-raising efforts combined with the multiplication of protean scandals, we have gone from "consume better as long as it doesn't ruin me" to "consume better, whatever the cost".

This paradigm shift is forcing companies to place at the heart of their activities, principles of action and values likely to provide their prospects and customers with an unambiguous view of the ethical aspects of the strategic positions they take.

In light of the recent events surrounding the COVID 19 pandemic, it seems that moralization has become a necessity for companies. Indeed, the health crisis caused by the Covid 19 pandemic has highlighted the fact that in this time of multiple crises, which is not likely to subside any time soon[29] , ethical companies have a better chance of maintaining and developing than those focused solely on the profit motive. During the crisis, socially responsible purchasing behaviour increased. This leads us to believe that, in the future, companies will have to incorporate social accountability mechanisms into their operations[30] , if they want to benefit from the purchasing preferences dictated by the SRC approach during periods that are now exceptional in name only. So, whether in industrialized or developing countries, there is an urgent need to consider the actions companies need to take to reduce their negative impacts and increase their capacity to have a positive impact on society. Given the economic vitality of under-industrialized countries, the natural course of events will soon see the companies that thrive there take on the same societal centrality as their counterparts in developed countries[31] . These companies will soon be "society's business", or these companies will soon be "companies' business". Whether one subscribes to one or the other of these visions, it remains undeniable that in industrializing countries, the majority of companies are subject to an inescapable obligation, the satisfaction of which requires them to learn how to mobilize non-dependent stakeholders more

---

[29] Cf. Speech by the French President, Emmanuel Macron, at the United Nations on the occasion of the 77ième Session of the General Assembly of the United Nations.
[30] See above.
[31] See this article on the mutability of the African economy.

effectively to achieve their economic objectives, while remaining ethical. In this quest, they generally rely on the entire social body of their locality. The driving forces behind these groups of individuals are often delighted to lend them a helping hand, because the social contribution of certain companies is such that they have become indispensable to general prosperity. As a result, ethical businesses, more than the wishful thinking of idealistic theorists, today appear to be the foundation on which tomorrow's economy in industrializing countries will rest.

However, from a normative point of view, while most theories and legislation converge on the necessity, indeed the urgency, of moralizing corporate life, the conclusions of work on the meaning of the relationship between ethics and corporate financial performance are far from unequivocal. Ethics have a cost, and profit maximization is the main source of motivation for entrepreneurs and the raison d'être of a business in the form of a commercial company[32]. Reforms or situations that jeopardize the achievement of this goal could affect investor appetite and jeopardize the progress and wealth creation for which business is the main provider. Companies will only move towards moralizing their practices if they have objective, verifiable data demonstrating the possibility of a positive interrelationship between ethics and increased profits. Hence the importance of this study in demonstrating a possible symbiosis between ethics and performance.

In Africa, research into the positive correlations between ethics and performance is still in its infancy. Studies in this area are almost non-existent. There are no unambiguous studies on the possible existence of a positive relationship between the moralization of economic life and business prosperity. Thus, the possibility of humanity's annihilation if the economy is not rapidly moralized is not in itself sufficient to encourage entrepreneurs to adopt ethical behavior. Only a clear and unequivocal demonstration of the direct positive impact of ethical behavior on the bottom line can encourage companies to moralize their behavior in the marketplace.

The first chapter sheds light on the key concepts used in the present work. The second chapter deals with the instability of ethics in economic theories. The third deals with the difficult apprehension of ethics by managerial sciences. The fourth presents an empirical review of the interrelationship between ethics and performance.

---

[32] Article 4 of the OHADA Uniform Act on Company Law and Economic Interest Groups (UDSGIE) defines a commercial company as an entity "created by two or more persons who agree, by contract, to allocate to an activity assets in cash or in kind, or industry, with the **aim of sharing the profit or benefiting from the economy which may result therefrom**. Partners undertake to contribute to losses under the conditions laid down in this Uniform Act". This definition is unambiguous as to the primarily economic aspect of the company.

CHAPTER I: CLARIFICATION OF KEY CONCEPTS

In this chapter, we will focus on the components of the notions of ethics (1), enterprise (2) and performance (3).

1. Ethical concepts

Axiology, the "domain of the good", encompasses morality, ethics and deontology. It is a theory of values that relies on arguments to judge or justify conduct in terms of norms, universal values or behavior corresponding to the attributes of virtue. By using these terms as yardsticks for evaluating ethics, the proponents of axiology have helped to establish a synonymy between virtue, norm and value in everyday language. These words are generally used interchangeably, which is problematic since their notional dimensions encompass very different realities.

To see this, we need only present the three main axiological theories, without making any a priori distinction between morality, ethics and deontology; then, for each of these theories, we will associate morality, ethics and deontology with their current meanings. These successive steps will enable us to define the meaning we will attribute to ethics in the context of our present work.

Most philosophers choose to develop a moral theory to characterize what we should do, and thus identify the domain of the good.

These moral theories can be grouped into families. The three main ones are:

➤ The ethics of consequences or consequentialist conceptions, one of the best-known variants of which is the utilitarianism promoted by John Stuart Mill[33] ;

➤ The ethics of duties or deontological conceptions or Kantian ethics put into form by Immanuel Kant[34] ;

➤ And virtue ethics, inspired by Aristotle[35] .

---

[33] John Stuart Mill, British philosopher, logician and economist.
[34] Immanuel Kant, German philosopher. Founder of transcendental idealism.
[35] Aristotle, ancient Greek philosopher and polymath

For consequentialists, the action we must perform is that which promotes the good: its consequences must be the best possible. In contrast, deontologicalists believe that what we do should be determined by a number of principles, such as "We must not bear false witness", "We must not make promises without the intention of keeping them", or "We must not cause gratuitous suffering to sentient beings". For them, there is no need to take into account the consequences of actions, since only their motive is likely to give an indication of their validity. For their part, proponents of virtue ethics invite individuals to turn their attention to the character of the virtuous agent. If the action under consideration is one that a virtuous man would have performed, then that action will be considered good.

Notwithstanding the apparent opposition between these different approaches, Ruwen OGIEN[36] and Christine TAPPOLET[37] , in their book entitled "The Concepts of Ethics", have attempted to reconcile them. In their view, it is perfectly possible to agree on what is right, while at the same time disagreeing on what must be done or what is obligatory.

In their view, the fact that two people agree on the goodness of a thing does not prevent them from disagreeing on how to implement it. To illustrate this, the authors use the following dialogue: "You and we may think that freedom of expression is a good," but you'll say "We must respect it! And we'll say "No. It must be promoted!"

Through this conciliation, the authors proved that to pass judgment on an action is, above all, to assert that the action in question possesses a certain value. Thus, the common assertion that freedom or friendship are "values" is one to be avoided. Values are not things. Rather, they are qualities attached to things, rather like size or color. To return to our previous illustration, it's wiser to assert that freedom or friendship possess a certain value than to assert that they themselves are values.

The advantage of this inversion of logics is that it clearly highlights certain characteristics of values, such as the fact that they are graduated, i.e. that they exist in the mode of "more or less" rather than "all or nothing".

We can also give two examples of opposing moral obligations: "We must promote what is good and we must respect what is good".

---

[36] Ruwen OGIEN, contemporary French libertarian philosopher, Director of research in philosophy at the CNRS.
[37] Christine TAPPOLET: Canadian philosopher, Director of the Centre de Recherche en Éthique -CRE Canada.

Just as it is advantageous to use the term "value" to single out the qualities of things, it is beneficial to use the term "norm" to refer to obligations. Norm" has a more encompassing meaning than "obligations", as it includes both prohibitions and permissions. Moreover, the use of the term "norm" in relation to a rule of behavior denotes the intention of the author of this description of the good in a given situation, to circumscribe as far as possible the ability of its addressees to act.

Indeed, standards seem to operate on an all-or-nothing basis. An action can be more or less successful, halfway unsuccessful or almost perfect. But there is no such thing as an action that is more or less forbidden, half-permitted or almost obligatory. An action is either permitted or not, forbidden or not, obligatory or not.

As far as virtues are concerned, they are nothing more than character traits. They assert that it is these that count morally, and not our actions or duties.

In the light of these elements, we can identify the respective fields of norms, values and virtues as follows:

-        We start from the evaluative (value), which we'll also call "axiological", from the Greek "axio", meaning what is worthwhile, what is good, to the normative (standard), which we'll also call "deontic", from the Greek "Déon", meaning obligatory. In short, this is the thesis that "**what is good is what one must do (or must desire)**". Here, what is good is seen as a given that must be respected. This is the position endorsed by many deontologists and neo-Kantians.

-        From normative (or deontic) to evaluative (or axiological). This is one of the readings of the thesis at the heart of consequentialism, which basically states: "**what we must do is what is good, or what is best**". Here, what is good is a variable to be evaluated by the agent.

-        From duty to virtue. Proponents of virtue generally consider that the main moral question is not **"what should I do?", but "what kind of person should I be?"**.

Having expressed these ideas in general terms, we can now go into more detail about consequentialist, deontological and virtue ethics theories.

Consequentialism is the ideology according to which an agent should perform an action only if, and only if, that action promotes the good. Before acting, he or she must constantly assess the impact of the action in question.

It follows from this definition that a just action (in the sense of an action that should be performed) is one whose consequences are the best. It embodies the idea that agents should constantly pursue the realization of the greatest possible good, or, more technically, "maximize" the good. This general theoretical constraint has been endorsed by many contemporary theories.

The best known is the classical utilitarianism of Bentham and Mill. This theory defends a hedonism of value. What should be promoted, according to this theory, is the greatest pleasure or happiness for the greatest number. Since happiness is deemed equivalent to pleasure and the absence of pain, classical utilitarianism asks us to maximize pleasure and minimize pain. More recent versions of utilitarianism are more concerned with satisfying preferences or promoting interests. Deontologists have also developed their own approach to these issues.

The best-known deontological theories are those of Kant and Ross[38] . In their purest versions, they prescribe that we should always respect certain moral principles or rules of action - such as keeping one's promises, not lying, not killing innocent people - whatever the consequences from an impartial or impersonal point of view[39] .

In this approach, good - such as keeping one's promises - would be strictly required, while evil - such as lying, torturing and killing - would remain constantly prohibited. As a result of this demand for rectitude in actions, the prohibitions on which it is based are supposed to remain in force even in cases where, by not respecting them, immense evils, massacres of innocents, interminable wars could be avoided, or the lot of all could be improved in considerable proportions. This is why we speak of absolute principles.

In short, for an agent, the deontological approach means performing an action if and only if that action is required by absolute moral principles, which apply regardless of the consequences that follow.

Anyone who has taken an interest in debates in moral philosophy will be familiar with the case of the unfortunate Jim, who was given the choice of either killing one innocent person or allowing twenty others, equally innocent, to be slaughtered by the militiamen of a dictatorship. In these debates, the deontologist is supposed to argue that Jim is forbidden to kill one innocent person in order to save a greater number, and the consequentialist is supposed to take the opposite view.

---

[38] William David Ross: April 15, 1877 - May 5, 1971, British philosopher
[39] Cova, Florian. "Emmanuel Kant et l'éthique des principes", Nicolas Journet ed, *La Morale. Éthique et sciences humaines*. Éditions Sciences Humaines, 2012, pp. 85-95.

Proponents of virtue ethics turn these two theories on their head. The genealogy of the contemporary approach to ethics can be found in a text by Elizabeth Anscombe published last century[40]. Drawing on the work of illustrious predecessors such as Aristotle and Thomas Aquinas[41], Elizabeth Anscombe advanced the presupposition that moral duty has no meaning in the context of the state, since in such spaces, the good is that which is imposed by a law or authority (the State, the King, or even God). Starting from the premise that the essence of moral duties is that they are self-generated by moral principles immanent to individuals, and likely to constitute the seat of absolute prohibitions that do not sit well with the "legi-centric" definitions of the good at work in contemporary states.

By virtue ethics, an agent must perform an action if and only if that action is what a virtuous agent would perform in those circumstances.

Of course, all these theories are subject to varying degrees of criticism, but from our point of view they are complementary. For a good life together, you can't strictly apply one theory or the other. Our aim here is to present their main characteristics, so as to better explain the foundations of what we mean by morality, ethics and deontology.

If we analyze these three theories according to today's general conception of morality, ethics and deontology, we can make the following connections:Morality is generally defined today as a set of rules of conduct considered to be absolutely valid, which enable us to differentiate between right and wrong, just and unjust, acceptable and unacceptable, and to which we should conform. This corresponds to the deontological vision we have just outlined.

- Ethics, on the other hand, is not seen as a set of specific values and principles, but rather as an argumentative reflection on the right thing to do. This is a consequentialist conception of morality.

- Today, deontology refers to a set of rules of behavior (character traits) that an agent must observe, generally speaking, in the course of his or her professional life (doctors, chartered accountants, auditors, etc.). This is a conception of ethics as a version of the virtues.

In the context of our work, our conception of ethics will be that of consequentialist ethics, in this case in the most recent versions where it is more a question of satisfying preferences or promoting interests while recognizing the existence of a minimum of rules

---

[40] G.E.M. Anscombe, 1958, Modern Moral Philosophy, in Philosophy 33 (124), Cambridge University Press, pp. 1-19; French translations by G. Ginvert and P. Ducray, "La philosophie morale moderne", in Klesis, No.9, 2008
[41] Saint *Thomas Aquinas:* 1225 - March 7, 1274, Italian philosopher and religious.

(rights). Thus, egoistic theories that call for each individual to maximize his or her own good to the detriment of that of others are excluded from the outset.

As previously mentioned, popularized by Jeremy Bentham and developed, albeit with substantial modifications, by John Stuart Mill over the course of the 18^e and 19^e centuries, utilitarianism is a doctrine that assigns as the goal of individual and collective action, the pursuit of maximum pleasure and minimum pain. Utility is the sole criterion for deciding objectively what should (or should not) be done in the field of human conduct and legislation. As the saying goes, to achieve "the **greatest happiness for the greatest number of men"**.

Applied to the organization, this means explicitly integrating the interests and expectations of multiple stakeholders (not just shareholders) into the organization's goals and strategies, in order to satisfy the greatest number. According to this perspective, the sole aim of the organization should not be to maximize profit, i.e. financial profitability. Increasingly, authors believe that the satisfaction of other stakeholders is not incompatible with the pursuit of profit, but rather a determining factor in maximizing it, or at least sustaining it.

2. Business concepts

According to France's National Institute for Statistics and Economic Studies (INSEE), since 2010 there have been two possible statistical approaches to understanding the company. The first, a historical approach, corresponds to a legal definition presented as a legal unit. The second, more recent approach, uses a definition based on economic criteria.

According to INSEE, a legal unit is a legal entity under public or private law that must be declared to the relevant authorities in order to exist. Today's business statistics system is based on this concept, and the vast majority of business statistics disseminated by INSEE use it.

Legal entities that can be analyzed under the prism of this concept can be:

- Or legal entities, whose existence is recognized by law independently of the persons or institutions that own or are members of them;

- In other words, individuals who, as self-employed persons, are able to carry on an economic activity.

In terms of their legal status, legal units can take a variety of forms. The applicable legislation sets out two main categories:

- Sole proprietorships: where the entrepreneur operates alone and on his own;

- Incorporated businesses/companies, with several shareholders (in this case, among others, we'll consider public limited companies (SA), limited liability companies (SARL) and economic interest groups (Groupement d'Intérêt Economique).

In addition to this classification based on the number of owners, companies can also be classified according to capital ownership.

So we have private companies (where the capital is in private hands), public companies (where the state can exercise a dominant influence), mixed economy companies (where private and public coexist) and associations, for example - where self-management reigns.

The INSEE's second approach to the definition of a company differs profoundly from this purely legal definition. Decree no. 2008-1354 of December 18, 2008, issued in application of French Law no. 2008-776 of August 4, 2008 on the modernization of the French economy (known as the LME), formalizes its existence. This text defines the enterprise as the smallest combination of legal units that constitutes *"an organizational unit for the production of goods and services that enjoys a certain degree of decision-making autonomy, in particular for the allocation of its current resources"*.

In practical terms, companies in the economic sense are constructed from the legal units of groups of companies. If the legal unit does not belong to a group, then the company is the legal unit. If it does belong to a group, then the company is the group.

According to INSEE, industrial companies, the companies we're interested in here, are those that manage to combine production factors (facilities, supplies, labor, knowledge) to produce material goods for the market.

For the Union des Industries et Métiers de la Métallurgie de France, industrial companies are companies of varying sizes that produce goods (concrete objects that they manufacture and market to consumers) or services (actions or services they offer, such as training, maintenance, etc.).

The definition used in the industrial census report is as follows: "A company is said to be industrial when it is equipped with technology, using both the capital factor (machines/tools, equipment and financial resources) and the human factor capable of transforming raw materials into a finished product".

What's special about these companies is that they bring together men and women who work together using financial and technical resources (machines and, above all, know-how). The synergy of these forces is geared towards customer satisfaction.

However, this satisfaction is only possible when the company, in its operations, takes into account the expectations of all the players in its supply chain, i.e. employees, trade unions, shareholders, suppliers, associations, the press and so on.

3. Notion of performance

Both the accomplishment of a process and the measurement of the results obtained, a company's performance is a tangible datum capable of edifying stakeholders on the success a company can boast. In the Larousse, the meaning of performance varies according to the field in which it is used. In physics, for example, it can be used to designate "all the qualities that characterize the performance that a motor vehicle, (or) an aircraft, is capable of exhibiting". This primary meaning highlights the fact that the vocation of this word is to enable its addressee to observe the high competence of the entities and things to which it refers. This connection with the prodigious is confirmed by the meaning attributed to it in the sporting world. Indeed, in the world of sport, the term performance and the qualifier that follows it, performant, are used to designate a positive result achieved by an athlete or a team.

The polysemy of this word makes it a "catch-all"[42] (Pesqueux 2021), encompassing both the idea of actions and that of state (final stage or result). In a classic, "managerial" approach, performance contains a triple idea:

➤ It's a result that represents the "level of achievement of objectives" (Alain Burlaud, 2009);

➤ It's an action, which implies real production, i.e. a process;

➤ It can be a success, as an attribute of performance, which induces a judgment, and therefore subjectivity.

The combination of these three functions shows that organizational performance is a link between allocation - in the sense that the achievement of results depends on the mobilization of stakeholders and the implementation of energy-intensive actions - and recovery, since one of the direct consequences of positive performance is an increase in profit. This constant

---

[42] Yvon Pesqueux, "De la performance", *Online course*, ID: 10670/1.q6bkgx

substitution between giving and receiving at work in high-performance companies means that performance can be defined as the willingness and ability to act according to a wide variety of optimality criteria in order to produce a result. However, it should be borne in mind that performance can sometimes refer both to the result and to the actions that enabled it to be achieved (Bourguignon, 1996).

In this way, performance management is simply the considered and organized implementation of all the processes, actions and resources likely to guarantee and/or increase a company's profitability (Cohanier, Lafage and Loiseau, 2010[43]). In practice, one of the most proven applications of this type of management is the process-based approach developed within the US Navy by Captain Market. According to this approach, performance management corresponds in practice to a process that consists in defining the mission - objective in classic organizational language - and the expected outputs, determining performance standards, linking budget to performance, reporting results, and ensuring the effective presence of mechanisms guaranteeing that managers are accountable for results[44] .

In a classic, traditional approach, performance is seen as an indicator of results. It refers to the notion of return on invested capital, the best-known indicator of which is R.O.I. (Return on Investment).

As we can easily subsume from its name, ROI is a financial indicator that measures the profitability that an economic agent can reasonably expect from a given investment. Because of their respective functions as a guide and a gauge of a company's performance, Performance Management and the ROI derived from it rely heavily on the concepts of effectiveness and efficiency, which appear as synonyms for performance, but sometimes also for the results to be achieved. In fact, it is preferable to refer to these notions rather than to productivity, which is more associated with an industrial approach, and therefore sometimes has negative connotations.

For De la Villarmois, efficiency could be defined as "the ability to achieve objectives[45] ". An effective company is one that is capable of doing what it set out to do, even if this means

---

[43] Bruno COHANIER, Philippe LAFAGE, Alain LOISEAU, Management de la Performance : des Représentations à la Mesure, 2010, IMTC.
[44] L. David MARQUET, Turn The Ship Around! A True Story of Turning Followers Into, Penguin Books Ltd, Paperback, October 8, 2015.
[45] De La VILLARMOIS, O. (2001). Le concept de performance et sa mesure, un état de l'art, Les Cahiers de la

allocating additional resources. As for efficiency, it introduces the notion of optimization into operational processes. For Drucker, effectiveness is about doing the right things, while efficiency is about doing things the right way[46].

Effectiveness represents the conformity of processes through which the initial objective has been achieved, while efficiency implies compliance with resource constraints, i.e. negotiated means (Commarmond and Exiga, 1998[47]). So, to be effective would mean to be both effective and efficient, in a given situation. Performance remains relative and context-dependent. What will be effective in one case will not necessarily be so in another (objectives revised upwards, different context...). For example, when a company forecasts sales by business unit, this forecast is based on the previous year's figures. And a simple change in the context (weather, external event, etc.) can be enough to cause the reference result to be missed.

These two notions are equally meaningful; they provide a liberal perspective on performance, which could then be seen as a metaphor for effectiveness and efficiency (Pesqueux). The model thus presents an image that is both simplified and practical (for communication purposes, for example) and incantatory (for rallying and remobilizing). Carlos Ghosn's postures and speeches in setting up Nissan's "revival plan" are a good illustration of this.

3.1. The liberal model, the dominant approach to performance

For liberals, the notion of performance is relative to the definition of objectives. Organizations can be conceived of as a whole focused on a goal: to do something specific. They are rational coordinations of activities set up to pursue explicit, and sometimes implicit, common goals and objectives (Schein 1971[48]). As demonstrated by Chester I Barrnard, The pursuit of a goal is even the condition of an organization's existence (Barabel, Michel 2017[49]). In the 1950s, an attempt was made to classify organizations according to their goals, which led to the development of a functionalist approach. Parsons sees the company as a living organism, and differentiates organizations according to the goals they pursue and the functions they perform.

Recherche, P. 1-21, 2001.

[46] Peter DRUCKER, Management: Tasks, Responsibilities, Practices, Harper Business, P.45-46, 1993.

[47] Alain Exiga, Gisèle Commarmond, Manager par les objectifs Fixer les objectifs, apprécier les résultats : les deux techniques essentielles du management, Ed. Eyrolles, Col. Fonctions de l'entreprise, 1998.

[48] Schein, E. H. (1971). "The Merger as Organizational Process", The Journal of Applied Behavioral Science, 7(1), pp. 110-111. https://doi.org/10.1177/002188637100700110

[49] Barabel, Michel. " I. Chester I. Barnard - L'organisation formelle ou l'art de la coopération", Sandra Charreire Petit ed, *Les Grands Auteurs en Management*. EMS Editions, 2017, pp. 11-28.

To summarize this approach, a global model can be presented, namely Gilbert's model (1980[50]), which is expressed through the performance triangle. Represented as follows:

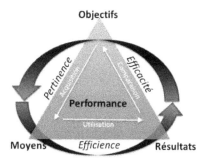

In this triangular model, the segment between objectives and results defines effectiveness, and indicates whether the company is sufficiently efficient to achieve its objectives. The segment between results and means defines efficiency, and indicates whether the company can achieve its objectives with fewer costs and resources. The segment between means and objectives defines relevance, and shows whether the company has equipped itself with the right means to achieve its objectives. This system is known as the "short-loop" system, and provides a simplified representation of the rational approach, giving pride of place to the basic notions of classical analysis.

The main dimension retained by the classical school is that of economic efficiency. This is expressed as the ratio between the quantity produced and the resources used to generate it. The stability of this measure poses a problem, as it is linked to the period of time represented. We're looking for reliability, validity and comparability. A good indicator will therefore be measurable, observable and controllable, but also simple, clearly defined and easy to understand.

Productivity plays a central role in the control mechanism. Originally, it was a physical concept that compared the units produced with the production factor used. This gives rise to a notion of relative performance, since productivity ratios enable us to compare ourselves with

[50] Carine Chemin and Patrick Gilbert, "L'évaluation de la performance, analyseur de la gouvernance associative The role of performance evaluation as an analyser of governance of associations", Politiques et management public Vol. 27, n°1, 2010, PP. 55-78.

the competitors of benchmark companies in the sector. Two types of inefficiency can be identified.

First, we would be inefficient compared to a competitor who produces as much with fewer resources. We would then be inefficient in relation to a competitor who produces more with the same resources (Parsons, 1994). Partial productivity indicators are frequently used by companies to overcome the limitations of financial indicators.

However, financial indicators have come to the fore with the development of the market economy and the pre-eminence of financial markets.

Without going into detail about the various financial tools, the internal growth of a company's business depends directly on the level of capital committed, and therefore on its ability to increase its economic assets. This means either increasing shareholders' equity or increasing financial debt. Profit, synonymous with earnings, would be the measure of accounting performance, since it shows the positive difference between the amount of sales of products or services and their cost of production or realization and distribution. Profitability, on the other hand, is a broader indicator that measures the margin differential obtained in relation to an accounting reference level for the business. It therefore represents a genuine indicator of the efficiency of capital employed. In this case, we look for an expected rate of profitability based on the level of competition or the sector of activity.

The creation of shareholder value has become the new credo of executives at major French and international companies. Recent developments concerning excessive executive remuneration through stock options illustrate this phenomenon. The creation of shareholder value has thus become the watchword over the last ten years, but the problem is how to measure it.

3.2. The limits of the liberal performance model

The authors of the classical and neoclassical schools of thought sought an objective approach to business, using a wide range of indicators. Above all, they sought to extract major principles of efficiency (see Filleau and Marques-Ripoull). Certainly, the economic success of certain models (Taylorism, Fordism) has demonstrated the validity of this approach. The Taylorian inspiration can still be felt in certain sectors (fast-food restaurants). As far as measurement itself is concerned, financial ratios have established themselves as genuine decision-making criteria. However, they have a number of limitations.

The first is the difficulty of measurement. Ranking companies according to the criterion of shareholder value creation presupposes a reliable, unchallengeable measurement tool. However, it is difficult to really know a company's weighted average cost of capital. Some researchers have shown that there are significant variations in the measurement of economic value creation, depending on the methodology used. For the same net operating profit, EVA varies according to a joint change in invested capital and the weighted average cost of capital.

This approach can also be criticized for being short-termist. There is a discrepancy between individual shareholders' desire to invest for the long term and the validity of EVA as an indicator. It remains an annual performance indicator, and there is nothing to suggest that it ensures a policy of long-term wealth creation.

An analysis of sustainable companies has shown that they have also been able to take human capital into account to a large extent. Performance is therefore no longer purely financial, but rather multi-dimensional, with the human factor a necessary consideration.

3.3. The multidimensional and contingent aspect of performance

Performance is both multidimensional and contingent. It is multidimensional because we can find different action variables and numerous criteria for assessing their relevance.

In fact, each school of thought adopts its own criteria of effectiveness and dimensions of analysis. Broadly speaking, research distinguishes four main dimensions that intersect depending on the company and the practitioner: social, economic, political and systemic.

The social approach focuses on the value of human resources and seeks to demonstrate their real added value. The economic approach, developed in the first part, is largely based on economic efficiency and seeks to measure productivity and compare indicators over time, in order to make decisions. The political approach focuses on the organization's legitimacy in relation to its stakeholders, and assesses their differentiated and antagonistic interests. It is not uncommon for managers to believe that a company is performing well, while employee representatives see it as a social step backwards. Finally, the systemic approach focuses on the company's ability to adapt to its environment, which will ensure its long-term survival. The shareholder/manager pairing is no longer the only relevant axis in today's corporate governance. Indeed, the fragmentation of shareholders and the diversity of other stakeholders call for other modes of analysis. Norton and Kaplan pioneered this approach with their famous "balance scorecard" model (1992). This is a set of financial and non-financial measures grouped into four clusters, each of which addresses a key performance issue: the financial cluster, to determine the company's image in the eyes of its shareholders; the customer cluster, to find out how customers perceive the company; the internal cluster, to understand the areas in which the company excels; and the innovation cluster, to analyze the areas for improvement that will create value.

In this work, performance analysis will focus primarily on financial performance.

This instability in notions of performance is also reflected in the ethics of economic theories.

CHAPTER II: THE INSTABILITY OF ETHICS IN ECONOMIC THEORY

Ethics is a moving concept. It has undergone constant evolution through the great currents of economic thought from the Middle Ages to the modern era.

1. The omnipresence of ethics in economic theory

The relationship between ethics and economics has undergone many vicissitudes over the ages. The philosophers of Greek antiquity and the theologians of the Middle Ages saw economics and morality as inseparable, while the mercantilists saw economics as separate from all moral and religious considerations. From the Industrial Revolution onwards, the opposition initiated by the mercantilists was subsequently exacerbated by the liberals. One thing leading to another, the economy went from being a means to happiness to an end in itself.

It's only in recent decades that this Manichean vision of the economy has begun to fade. In the wake of repeated scandals, recurring crises and the negative impact of economic life on society and the environment, we are witnessing the return of ethics to economic theory. One of the most illustrious proponents of this current of thought is India's Amartya Sen, who summed up his moral vision of economics in his book, aptly entitled Economics is a Moral Science. His reflections throughout this work focus on the consubstantiality of ethics and economics. For the author, the only viable economy in today's society is one that makes the reinforcement of equity in the distribution of services and wealth the tautological goal of any society. SEN's work is the culmination of several centuries of evolution in the relationship between ethics and economics.

1.1. The beginnings of the moral economy

Although Hammurabi's code contains a few economic notions (prices and wages)[51] , it was not until the works of Plato and Aristotle that economic thinking became explicit among Greek philosophers, who studied domestic economics and city management.

However, it was Xenophon, a disciple of Plato and thus of Socrates, who first coined the word "economy", derived from the Greek words "*oikos*" and "nomos", meaning "house" and "rules" of life respectively. Economy would therefore be the set of rules governing domestic activities.

---

[51] For example, paragraph 60.

It's worth remembering that at that time, most of man's activities took place in the home. There was no industry or market in the modern sense. In Xenophon's view, women were responsible for the upkeep of the home (oikos), while politics were a matter for men and work for slaves.

As far as Plato and Aristotle are concerned, there are two questions concerning the economy that will be the subject of debate between them. The first is the question of property: should it be collective, as Plato thinks, or private, as Aristotle maintains?

Plato approaches economics as the management of goods and people in the fairest possible way. Aristotle, on the other hand, refutes this Platonic communism. For him, common ownership of land leads to inefficient management, as it is no longer possible to ensure that each person's remuneration is proportional to his or her contribution: "As work and enjoyment are not equally distributed, claims will necessarily arise against those who enjoy or receive much, while working little, on the part of those who receive little, while working much[52]". The modernity of Aristotelian thought that emerges from this emblematic passage of *Politics* is even more apparent when he writes, for example, that: "*Putting everything in common is the most difficult undertaking of all for man*". Here, the illustrious thinker points out that property owned in joint ownership generates far more conflict than that owned separately. For him, the best form of property is individual ownership, which is the only way to achieve human fulfillment. Moreover, Aristotle considered a certain amount of material wealth to be necessary for well-being, as "*Happiness cannot do without external goods. [(yet)...] It is impossible, or at least difficult, to do well if one lacks the resources[53]*".

The second economic question that gave rise to controversy between Plato and Aristotle concerned the distribution of wealth: should it be distributed egalitarily, as Plato demands, or should it be distributed in proportion to individual effort, as Aristotle will explain?

Aristotle believes that equality does not mean giving everyone the same thing, but rather ensuring that everyone receives a share in proportion to their efforts. This is what he calls distributive justice. In economic terms, justice manifests itself in commercial exchanges according to the following principle: The thing received must be equivalent to the thing given in exchange. The author calls this form of justice commutative justice.

---

[52] Aristotle, Politics, L. II, ch. 2.
[53] Aristotle, Nicomachean Ethics, I, VIII, 15.

These debates make Plato the forerunner of communism, and Aristotle the forerunner of liberalism. Aristotle divided the science of man into three branches: Ethics, Economics and Politics. While Ethics concerns the individual and Politics the city, Economics characterizes family activity. Both have contempt for profit, but they express it differently.

For Plato, the idea of profit is contemptuously rejected by the lower classes of society, such as slaves, foreigners and merchants. Aristotle, on the other hand, uses a particular rhetoric to talk about profit and the acquisition of wealth. He speaks of chrematistics, the word by which he designates activities that consist in the acquisition of goods. According to Aristotle, there are two forms of chrematistics (i.e., the acquisition of wealth): a natural and legitimate one, and a low and reprehensible one.

The natural and legitimate form is that of acquiring goods to satisfy one's needs. In other words, farming, animal husbandry, fishing and hunting. The lower, condemnable form is commercial activity - and not all commercial activity, but only that part of commercial activity which is carried out not to satisfy needs, but to make a profit from it. In other words, a peasant who goes to sell his harvest at market and comes back with clothes and spices is engaging in trade which is not condemnable, but someone who buys wheat from a peasant and sells that wheat for a profit is condemnable. He is even more reprehensible if he takes advantage of the scarcity of wheat to raise the price, or if he stocks wheat in the hope of raising the price.

Subsequently, Saint Thomas Aquinas, reflecting on Aristotle's thought, largely adopted the Greek thinker's ideas and attempted to reconcile the economic and the religious.

1.2.   The advent of the moral economy

In the Middle Ages, Christian morality inspired economic thought, notably that of **Saint Augustine** and **Saint Thomas Aquinas**.

The Church inherited from ancient philosophy the economic principle that exchange in itself is sterile. As a result, believers at the time had a negative attitude towards economics. This negative perception was reinforced by Christianity, which took up the philosophical idea of the danger of wealth, of chrematistics: to produce in order to live and to make others live, nothing could be more legitimate says Saint Thomas Aquinas, but to produce for the sole purpose of earning more is a sin[54] . Guided by such principles, the Church gradually turned to an economic

---

[54] See Sivéry, Gérard. "La notion économique de l'usure selon saint Thomas d'Aquin", Revue du Nord, vol. 356-

policy of spending rather than profit. Unable to turn to commercial activity, it will devote its works to charity and the glory of God. Charity dictated that the monasteries' economy should not produce, but rather earn in order to give, and thus to produce with a view to spending[55]. The charity of the faithful was essentially focused on assisting the sick, helping captives and abandoned children, and most often led to the distribution of home help and the building of hospitals.

Guided by these same principles, the Church took clear and firm positions on certain aspects of economic life. The Church's moral concerns led it, for example, in a theorization due to Saint Thomas, to advocate the right price "which should vary neither with supply and momentary demand, nor with individual caprice, nor with the skill of haggling". The moral duty of both buyer and seller is to seek to approach this fair price as closely as possible. This notion of a fair price is correlated with that of a fair wage. Here, theologians are in line with the preoccupations of city rulers and guild masters, who were guided by public order rather than spiritual motives.

Since the purpose of work is not to produce excessively, but to produce in order to live; since the purpose of life is not to produce, but to earn one's salvation; religion takes precedence, if we dare use this shortcut, over productivity. In this way, "sacred unemployment" sets in. Because of the number of feasts and vigils, the average working week in the 12th century was hardly more than four days. In the 15th century, a good number of public holidays were abolished, but by the 17th century, there were almost a hundred without Sundays included in the count.

Thus, the Gospels teach that no human being can serve both God and money (Mt 6:24; Lk 16:13), and that "it is easier for a camel to go through the eye of a needle than for a rich man to enter the Kingdom of God." (Lk 18. 25)

However, Protestantism was to mark a break in the perception of work and wealth. In 1905, in his book "Protestant Ethics and the Spirit of Capitalism", Max Weber used a two-stage approach to emphasize the fundamental role played by Protestantism in economic development. Firstly, he noted that the Protestant religion valued work, whereas Catholicism equated it with punishment. Secondly, he revealed that the Reformed religion (Protestantism) condemned poverty. Where Catholics appealed to Christian charity, Protestants saw helping the poor as a

---

357, no. 3-4, 2004, pp. 697-708.
[55] Saint Thomas Aquinas, Summa Theologica, Part.2, article 12, page 83 ff.

stimulus to idleness. For Protestants, the right thing to do was to give work to the beggar, rather than offering him a trifle as alms. Wealth is valued as a token of the economic orientation of Protestantism, and is portrayed as a sign of predestination, the work of an intense spiritual life. As with any divine blessing, wealth can be a source of calamity if it is used to corrupt rather than to perfect actions and activities that are appreciated by the divine, but it must be used correctly. To avoid this, the theologian advocates devoting the economy to fair trade, savings and productive investment, and relegating to the background, or even annihilating, its over-consumption dimension and unbridled quest for pleasures56 . Thus, in the economic model derived from Protestant theology, the entrepreneur is seen as indispensable, since his activity demonstrates piety, righteousness and faith. By basing his livelihood on the product of his work and investments, and by creating jobs for others, the entrepreneur demonstrates the qualities of the pious[57] .

2. The decline of the moral economy

It was during the Renaissance that a theoretical break was made in the idea of wealth accumulation.

In contrast to the medieval concept of money and wealth, late Renaissance writers such as Montchrestien (1576-1621) advocated the accumulation of precious metals. The idea was not to sell a commodity at its "fair price", but to obtain as much silver or gold as possible. The economy thus freed itself from the ethical concerns that had been consubstantially linked to it since antiquity and the Middle Ages. Generally speaking, mercantilism is a doctrine of state accumulation of precious metals and an incentive to produce wealth. The proponents of this policy can be divided into three mercantilist currents: Spanish (Bullionism), French (Colbertian industrialism) and English (Commercialism).

While Spanish mercantilism was not developed in a theoretical way, both English and French mercantilism were conceptualized before imprinting lasting trends on the economic and financial practice of these two nations.

---

[56] Saint Thomas Aquinas, Summa Theologica, Part.2, article 4, Question 77, page 316 ff.
[57] According to St. Augustine, reported by St. Thomas Aquinas in Summa Theologica, the pious person is one who shows mercy to his neighbor, for "the word piety is still used by the people to designate works of mercy [meaning of this word which would come from the fact that] God particularly recommends such works, declaring that they are as much and more pleasing to him than sacrifices."

In the British Empire, the emergence of mercantilism is largely attributable to Thomas Mun (1571-1641) and his Discourse on Commerce (1621), as well as Josiah Child and his Brief Observations on Commerce (1688). This trend, which considered foreign trade to be the most resource-generating activity, equated money with capital and made it the driving force behind commercial exchanges.

For its part, French mercantilism is often equated with Colbertism: economic policy consists of developing manufacturing activity in order to accumulate precious metals. This idea is present in Laffemas's treatise on the history of commerce (1545-1612), but is reinforced by Antoine de Montchrestien's treatise on political economy (1615). Subsequently, it fell to Colbert to put this into practice by promoting "high value-added" industrial activity, if necessary through protectionist measures, by attracting specialties from other countries[58] . This competition is designed to supplant the industries of other countries, and its ultimate aim remains the draining of precious metals from other countries.

In France, for example, advances in machinery and the means of communication, together with the system of property ownership established by the Civil Code of 1804[59] , led to unprecedented growth in economic life, which eventually evolved into competitive capitalism based on freedom of enterprise. This evolution was made possible by the emergence of liberalism, which took shape in the 17th and 18th centuries with Locke, Montesquieu and Adam Smith, continuing and modifying the work of the pioneers of modern thought (Machiavelli and Hobbes in particular). Their work in deconstructing pre-existing models was remarkably successful at the time, to such an extent that the principles they disseminated served as the foundation for the young American Republic[60] . But before the development of this current, a brief economic movement called physiocracy appeared in the 18th century.

2.1. Agriculture as the only source of wealth

Physiocracy, whose leader was François Quesnay (1694-1774), had illustrious supporters including Catherine II of Russia and King Stanislas II of Poland. This current was in opposition to the ideas defended by the mercantilists. Firstly, the physiocrats were hostile to

---

[58] Minard, Philippe. "Economie de marché et Etat en France: mythes et légendes du colbertisme", *L'Économie politique*, vol. 37, no. 1, 2008, pp. 77-94.
[59] Article 544 of this Code stipulated that "ownership is the right to enjoy and dispose of things in the most absolute manner, provided they are not used in a way prohibited by laws or regulations".
[60]

state intervention, whereas the mercantilists were in favor of it. Secondly, the most striking dividing line between these two currents is the true nature of enrichment. For the older of the two, mercantilism, enrichment is above all monetary - the more money or jewels you have, the richer you are - whereas for the more recent, true enrichment is agricultural. For the physiocrats, strongly inspired by the structure of the medieval French economy, only agriculture was capable of producing a surplus beyond the materials used, i.e., a net product that was the initial capital enabling the national economy to function[61] . Manufacturing, on the other hand, is sterile, as it is unable to generate any net product. In their view, while it transforms wealth, it does not create it.

With the physiocrats, wealth became material, not just monetary, as the mercantilists had claimed. Of course, the economic thinking of the physiocrats should not be seen as being based solely on the mechanisms of maximizing net agricultural product. Such a reduction would be a mistake, as this school of thought abounds in interesting reflections on all aspects of economics. To see this, we need only dwell on Quesnay's writings on the interdependence of the sources of wealth of different types of economic agents.

The physiocrats, like the early liberals, believed that the state should not interfere in the economy, and should respect the physical laws that guide it. Individual interests, especially those of farmers, are in line with the general interest. The natural order of the economy and private property must be respected. The physiocrats were thus the first liberals to advocate material and non-monetary enrichment, and above all to create the first economic circuit between three classes: the productive class (farmers), the proprietary class (landowners) and the sterile class (other citizens occupied with other services and drawing their income from the other two classes).

This economic liberalism can be illustrated by the famous phrase coined by the physiocrat Vincent de Gournay: "laissez faire les hommes, laissez passer les marchandises" ("let men do, let goods pass"). It indicates that the state should not intervene, and that no obstacles to the circulation of goods should be erected. This idea is echoed in Adam Smith's "invisible hand" principle. According to this principle, every individual who pursues a purely individual, even selfish, interest is working for the collective interest, or general prosperity.

---

[61] Charbit, Yves. "The political failure of an economic theory: physiocracy", *Population*, vol. 57, no. 6, 2002, pp. 849-878.

2.2.   The economy as a space for individualistic wealth accumulation

The industrial revolution of the 18th century gave rise to liberalism, a new school of thought that would become the foundation of modern economic thought. This new approach to economics is generally divided into two schools: the classical and the modern.

The classical school spans the period from 1776, the date of Adam Smith's masterwork, Research into the Nature and Causes of the Wealth of Nations, to 1848, the date of John Locke's Principles of Political Economy. The main ideas of the classical school were the harmony of individual interests, respect for the natural order and the need for the state to refrain from intervening in the economy.

But the Industrial Revolution was not just the fruit of economic phenomena; it also had its roots in the political ideas and events of the 17th century. In 1688, England's "Glorious Revolution" gave the country a parliamentary monarchy. The ensuing upheavals were brilliantly documented by John Locke (1632-1704), considered the father of liberalism. Indeed, the parliamentary monarchy gave power to the great landowners, who implemented policies enabling them to make the most of their estates. A tax based on the size of the estate was introduced, to avoid taxing farmers in proportion to their harvests, which would have a demotivating effect. With its roots in liberalism, the Industrial Revolution gave rise to capitalism. For John Locke, men had "natural rights": liberty, property, security. Social harmony would result from the use of freedom by individuals in the service of their property.

Subsequently, John Locke advocated what Leo Strauss called "capitalist hedonism", which he summarized as follows: "the greatest happiness consists not in enjoying the greatest pleasures, but in possessing the things that produce the greatest pleasures". Possession and production are therefore at the heart of liberalism.

Adam Smith (1723-1790), the founder of modern liberalism, considered man to be a being who seeks sympathy and approval for his behavior from those closest to him. In this respect, a strong, authoritarian state is unnecessary, as there is little asocial behavior to curb. Contrary to the mercantilists, Smith postulates that true wealth is not gold, but the product that can be consumed. Wealth therefore comes from material production; the aim of Smith's work is precisely to determine the means of increasing this production in order to enrich the nation.

The first way to increase production is to divide labor. With his famous example of the pin factory, Smith shows that labor is the main factor in increasing productivity.

The second way to enrich the nation is to let individuals enrich themselves, because by working in their own self-interest, they unintentionally enrich the nation as a whole: this is the famous notion of the "invisible hand". On this subject, Smith would say that "it is not from the benevolence of the butcher, the beer merchant, or the baker, that we expect our dinner, but from the care they take of their interests. We address ourselves not to their humanism, but to their egoism[62] (...) Each individual constantly puts all his efforts into finding the most advantageous use for all the capital at his disposal; he thinks only of his own gain: in this, as in many other cases, he is led by an invisible hand to fulfill an end which is not at all in his intentions. While seeking only his personal interest, he often works far more effectively for the interest of society, than if his aim were really to work for it."

Indeed, to get rich, people had to produce, create industries and therefore hire. This desire to get rich is certainly the main cause of the Industrial Revolution and the reason for the British advance. Indeed, whereas in 18th-century France the main motivation for many nobles was the social prestige associated with the king's favors, many Britons sought to enrich themselves.

The classical school therefore advocates first and foremost respect for the natural order, although for Mill, considered the last classical author, the existence of the invisible hand is questionable insofar as the interest of the strongest may prevail and inequalities exist. He adheres to general principles such as utilitarianism and laissez-faire, but nevertheless accepts state intervention in the social sphere and advocates a certain social reformism.

The neoclassical school, an extension of this school, observed that "the XIXe century ended with a cruel contradiction: scientific and industrial progress failed to resolve the social question". The opinion conveyed by classical political economy is contradicted by the facts: economic development has certainly led to an increase in national wealth, but it has not in itself brought about an improvement in the living conditions of the working classes. John Maynard Keynes (1883-1946), whose theories captured the attention of economists throughout the second half of the 19th^e century, referred to this state of affairs in his book, General Theory of Employment, as "the paradox of poverty in the midst of plenty".

---

[62] Adam Smith (1776), Investigations into the Nature and Causes of the Wealth of Nations: Volume I, Chapter II, P. 23 available online

In France, Léon Walras (1834-1910) was struck by this unfortunate coexistence, to such an extent that he attempted to reconcile liberalism and justice through the notion of justice[63]. In England, at the same time, Alfred Marshall (1842-1924) saw it in the light of another cultural tradition. The social question, at the heart of Marshall's theoretical project, is interpreted through the notion of well-being, in a perspective that is genetically articulated, but not subservient to utilitarianism. "The spirit of the age prompts us to examine more carefully the question whether our increasing wealth might not serve, more than it does, to develop the general welfare, and in the first place, that of the poorest" A. Marshall (1920), Principles of Economics.

As far as the conception of the purpose of economic science is concerned, the neoclassical school marks a break in the evolution of theory, contrary to what the prefix "neo" implies. Whereas economics had hitherto been the science of wealth accumulation, it became the science of scarcity and resource allocation, as defined by Lionel Robbins (1932), and based on a new conception of value, and a microeconomic approach in terms of market equilibrium. However, like the classics, neoclassicals are generally advocates of economic liberalism and its corollary, economic individualism.

The monetarists, or ultraliberals, took neoclassical reasoning to the extreme, purging the economy of all considerations not geared to profit maximization. The initiator of this trend, Milton Friedman (1912-2006)[64] based his theories on the quantitative theory developed by Irving Fisher (1867-1947), an American economist and mathematician. His motto, which sums up his purely capitalist vision of the economy, was: "The business of business is business. For him, "a company's only social responsibility is to increase its profit". However, his attempt to exclude all ethical considerations from the economy came up against an insurmountable logical obstacle. His liberal postulate that the company is under no obligation to society breaks down when market mechanisms require it to return part of its assets to society. This is the case when the company's ethical character becomes a predominant criterion in triggering customers' purchasing decisions. Indeed, in such a situation, his assertion - to demonstrate the self-regulating nature of the market - that if customers aren't satisfied, they'll buy elsewhere - requires companies to be more ethical if they are to survive and make a profit. So, by seeking

---

[63] Lacan, Arnaud. "Léon Walras and mutual insurance companies", *RECMA,* vol. 299, no. 1, 2006, pp. 6882.
[64] Friedman was an American economist specializing in monetary issues. He was the founder of the monetarist movement (also known as the Chicago School).

to exclude ethics from the economy, ultraliberalism merely keeps them there. In this respect, it is in line with Keynesian thinking.

3. On the revival of moral economics

Thanks to the expansion of Keynesian thinking in the second half of the 19th^e century, ethics found its way into economic thinking (**3.1**) **as the** essential notion it is today (**3.2**): moral economics as the only alternative to decline.

3.1. The economy as a factor of social equality

John Maynard Keynes (1883-1946) was a British economist and civil servant whose analyses revolutionized economic theory and policy.

Keynesian theory, while remaining within the framework of the market economy, is strongly opposed to neo-classical theory, and justifies the need for state intervention in the face of economic crises. This theory is presented in Keynes's major work, "The General Theory of Employment, Interest and Money", published in 1936.

Keynes immediately took a macroeconomic perspective. However, he was fundamentally concerned with ethics. Inspired by Aristotle, who proposed a division of the science of man into three branches: Ethics, Economics and Politics, Keynes said that "economics, politics and ethics are the three passengers in a car, adding that it is not economics that should be at the wheel. But at present, in most countries, economic forces are de facto allowed to solve the problems, because politicians have no project to propose to the population. We've reached the point where it's almost shameful to say we're taking an ethical stand! But we'll have to put ethics back in its place if we don't want our society to become a jungle where, at the slightest accident, everyone risks tipping over into this dangerous zone where they are no longer of interest to the economic world".

The return of ethics to economic thinking, foreseeable as early as the 1930s due to the influence of Keynesianism, reached its peak with the irruption of Marxism in Western societies.

Strictly speaking, Marxism can be defined as the set of theses expounded by the German philosopher Karl Marx (1818-1883).

According to Marx, capitalist society is founded on an economic and social organization characterized by the opposition of two antagonistic classes: on one side are those who own the means of production (the bourgeoisie or capitalists), and who dominate and exploit those on the other side, the working class (the proletarians), whose only asset is their "labor power". For Marx, the instigator of this opposition is private ownership of the means of production.

According to Marxist theory, in the capitalist system, the labor capacity of proletarians is a mere commodity like any other that can be offered for purchase. Marx despised this system because he believed that proletarians were being robbed. Indeed, Marx, like certain classical economists such as Ricardo, considered labor to be the sole source of the value of goods produced. For him, the difference between the amount of labor provided by workers and the amount of labor just required to pay their wages - surplus value - instead of accruing to its natural beneficiaries - the proletarians - reverted to investors - the capitalists - thus maintaining a one-way relationship of dependence that had no place in the human society he was fomenting, despite his awareness of its utopian nature.

Although Marxism has been the foundation of certain political regimes for which ethics was a superfluous principle of government[65] , it is at the origin of modern economic thought, which makes ethics the guiding principle of a significant proportion of individuals' economic interactions.

3.2.   The moral economy as the only alternative to decline

As mentioned in the introduction to this section, over the last few decades we have witnessed the necessary return of ethics to economic theory. This trend of thought is championed by Amartya Sen and summarized in his book Economics is a Moral Science. In essence, Sen inserts an ethical dimension into economics, revealing that the economy was merely a means to a more just human society, and that it would never be considered the tautological goal of any society. Ethics have become a central element in managerial theories.

---

65 André Piettre, Marx et marxisme, Presses universitaires de France, 1966, p. 168.

CHAPTER III: THE DIFFICULTY OF UNDERSTANDING ETHICS IN MANAGERIAL SCIENCE

The company, an essential economic player, has long been reduced by economic theory to a single rational agent seeking to maximize profit. Economists have gradually turned their attention to this black box and the actions and relationships that take place within it. Their work has both enriched traditional economic theory and paved the way for new economic and sociological analyses of organizations.

For a long time, only neo-classical theory provided an economic representation of the company. The producer faced the consumer, the company became one with the entrepreneur, and the latter sought to maximize profit by using a certain combination of production factors. However, while this model was intended to describe the role and interest of the market, it did not provide any analysis of the internal workings of a company. Far from being a black box, a company is made up of players who work, exchange with each other and with the outside world, sometimes clash, etc. This is why many economists and economists of the past have taken up the idea of the market as a means of maximizing profit. As a result, many economists and sociologists began to analyze what goes on in and around the company.

The first theories sought to justify the existence of firms, before the others looked in depth at ways of improving their efficiency. The ethical dimension occupies an important place in each of these theories.

1. The penetration of ethics into technology

1.1. Transaction cost theory

Transaction cost theory has been developed in several stages. In its current developments, it is based on certain assumptions that differ from neoclassical axiomatics, principally an assumption of different rationality.

The concept of transaction cost was first introduced by Ronald Coase in 1937. For many years, there was no commentary on the concept, but it did earn its author some belated fame (Nobel Prize in 1991). It was thanks to Williamson's work that the notion of transaction cost came into its own. Thanks to this concept, transaction cost theory is able to account for the existence of the firm in a market economy.

Unlike property rights or agency theory, transaction cost theory does not aim to demonstrate the superiority of the capitalist firm over any other form of production organization. The question Coase intends to answer is that of the existence of the firm.

Why do companies exist in a market economy?

In an attempt to explain this way of coordinating production, Coase introduced a concept that would lay the foundations of organizational science: organizational efficiency. An economic organization is efficient when it minimizes operating costs. These operating costs are called transaction costs. The unit of analysis is the transaction. This is always the subject of a contract, the nature of which characterizes a specific form of organization.

For Coase, the firm is defined as a relationship of authority. The firm brings asymmetrical contracts into play, insofar as employees freely accept subordination to the employer's will. This is in contrast to market relations. In such a mode of coordination, agents are deemed symmetrical, and there is no relationship of power or subordination.

O.E. Williamson completes the work begun by Coase by adding heterodox hypotheses, in the sense that they diverge from the neoclassical axiomatics to which Coase does not deviate in his work. Williamson thus proposes a comprehensive theory of transaction organization that accepts two extremes: the firm and the market. The main hypotheses concern the behavior of the economic agent, whom Williamson calls Homo contractor.

- Bounded rationality

It's a concept borrowed from Herbert Simon. Limited" should be understood not in the sense of "irrational", but in the sense that individuals do not have all the elements they need to make a purely rational choice, i.e. one that considers all possible solutions. This forces them to fall back on solutions that seem "reasonable" or "satisfactory". This is why we sometimes speak of "satisficing" instead of "maximizing".

To this assumption about the cognitive abilities of individuals, Williamson adds that of opportunism, more precisely the opportunism of agents.

Opportunism is "a pursuit of self-interest that involves the notion of deception". For Williamson, opportunistic behavior consists of "making individual gains in transactions through a lack of candor or honesty."

Opportunism is part of human nature, and corresponds to the strategic behavior of agents who seek their own strictly personal interest, even if this means harming the other party to the contract, by resorting to cunning, bad faith, lies, cheating, etc... Williamson distinguishes two types of opportunism: anti-selection and moral chance.

Ex ante opportunism

Occurs when there is cheating before a contract is concluded between the parties. Example: communication of erroneous information by a seller. This opportunism is possible because of the asymmetry of information due to the specificity of human assets. This opportunism brings us back to the problem of anti-selection.

Ex post opportunism

Occurs when there is cheating in the execution of the contract, or at the end of the contract (evaluation of the parties' actions, question of contract renewal). This opportunism is linked to the incompleteness of contracts and limited rationality, but also to the specificity of assets. This opportunism brings us back to the problem of moral hazard.

The opportunism hypothesis doesn't mean that all agents are opportunistic; it means that they all can be, because individuals are all expected to pursue their own self-interest. Consequently, opportunism introduces suspicion, doubt and, more generally, behavioral uncertainty. This uncertainty introduces another linked to the stability of opportunistic behavior over time: we can't know in advance what the behavior of others will be. The introduction of time - transactions are carried out over time - makes the execution of contracts susceptible to opportunism. Indeed, if transactions were unwound instantaneously, there would be no problem of opportunism. The introduction of time and its implicit consideration in the model means that we no longer speak of exchange, but of transaction.

Williamson's emphasis on contracts and the economic analysis of law makes his work a multi-disciplinary endeavor, but it is worth emphasizing the influence of North American economics, particularly in terms of competition and antitrust law. It can be said that transaction cost economics marks a break with neoclassical economic doctrine, and is part of a movement to "renew microeconomics through a detailed analysis of individual behaviour and the interactions between these behaviours" (Coriat and Weinstein, 1995). The notion of opportunism is also found in agency theory.

1.2. Agency theory

When shareholders hire a manager, the risk for them is that this manager will decide according to his or her own interests (growing the company by reinvesting all profits, for example) and not respect the shareholders' objectives (paying high dividends). Similarly, managers are concerned about opportunistic behavior on the part of their employees.

The theory of property rights and the theory of agency then study the different ways of avoiding these situations linked to information asymmetries.

The theory of property rights shows that every market relationship is an exchange of property rights over goods or services. Thus, owning an asset (such as a business) means owning the right to earn income from it, such as the right to use or sell it. But it also means the right to control how the asset is used - in other words, the right to make all the decisions for a business. As a result, there is no room for autonomy on the part of a company's executive managers. It is the shareholders who decide, even if they delegate their power to managers. It remains to be seen how they can control the latter or direct their behavior.

Agency theory studies the incentive systems that help answer these questions.

Adam Smith (1723-1790) had already addressed the issue: "The directors of these kinds of companies being stewards of other people's money rather than of their own, they can hardly be expected to bring to it that exact and solicitous vigilance which the partners of a company often bring to the handling of their funds." But it wasn't until 1976 that two authors, Jensen and Meckling, gave this theory its recognized definition:

"We define an agency relationship as a contract by which one or more persons (the principal) engage another person (the agent) to perform on their behalf some task which involves a delegation of some decision-making power to the agent."

Francophone purists prefer the terms mandant (rather than principal), mandataire (rather than agent) and relation de mandat (rather than agence).

According to this theory, the "agent" is the one who receives a mandate or who must carry out certain operations on behalf of another, the "principal". For example, in a company, the relationship between the manager and the shareholder, or between the manager and the employees, is an agency relationship. In this relationship, also known as an agency relationship or "principal-agent relationship", the situation of one depends on the situation of the other. Of course, there may be "negative incentives" in the form of controls, surveillance or sanctions, but these are sometimes too costly or ineffective. Individualized salaries, performance-related bonuses, profit-sharing, stock options, etc. are just some of the "positive" incentives designed to avoid divergences of interest or the consequences of information asymmetries between the parties.

The analyses developed by agency theory have fuelled debates on corporate governance, the main theme of which concerns relations between shareholders and managers.

In the 1930s, two American economists, Adolph Berle and Gardiner C. Means, showed that the dispersion of shareholders and the complexity of corporate management led to a dissociation between shareholders and managers, who could then follow their own interests. The return of shareholders since the 1980s, changes in financial systems (e.g. the growing role of savings funds, share price volatility) and the numerous bankruptcies of large companies (Enron and Worldcom in the USA) have highlighted the need for better guidance of managers' actions. Beyond this shareholder-manager relationship, some practitioners and theorists have turned their attention to the operational organization of work to boost productivity.

1.3.   The theory of scientific organization of work - OST

In economics, work is an activity that is remunerated. Along with capital, labor is a factor of production. It is, however, simplistic to summarize human intervention in the production process in terms of a single, abstract "factor", since both tasks and individuals have extremely varied characteristics. What's more, the most important element is the organization of work, i.e. the way in which activity is distributed among the company's various employees.

The English economist Adam Smith was the first to demonstrate the benefits of division of labor and specialization within the company (the "factory") to increase productivity.

Later, the American engineer Frederic Winslow Taylor (1856-1915), who had previously been a worker, developed what he called a scientific method of work organization (his book, published in 1911, is entitled "Scientific Management of Companies"). He criticized the traditional organization of work, in which skilled production workers predominated, autonomous and in control of their own time and activity, thanks to their know-how. For Taylor, productivity could only be improved by better control over the actual activity of these workers. He then set out the main principles of his Scientific Organization of Work (SOW).

The basis of his system is the scientific analysis of movements, times and pauses. The elimination of useless gestures, the breakdown of operations and the analysis of the tools used should make it possible to find the most efficient production method for each worker, the one best way. Taylor thus proposed a horizontal division of labor, with each worker assigned a few clearly-defined elementary tasks.

From the 1910s onwards, Henry Ford (1863-1947) continued Taylor's work by adding the assembly line system to the OST, i.e. the use of a mechanized "conveyor" to transport workpieces from one workstation to another. It's no longer the workers who move around, but the parts themselves, reducing downtime and the need for handling personnel. In addition, the chain increases the rate of production, as it sets the pace for the workers.

Taylor's original aim was altruistic. In his view, the interests of the boss (to produce at the lowest cost and make a profit) and the worker (to earn the best salary with the least effort) converged. To this end, he advocated that remuneration should be proportional to performance.

However, by focusing his analysis of the organization on the technical function, Taylor overlooks the fact that the company is a human organization where sociological and psychological aspects must be taken into account.

Several surveys carried out by sociologists in the 1930s showed that OST's mechanistic vision was too simplistic, and that workers' "morale" had a decisive influence on performance.

Today, Taylorism is being called into question once again by general economic changes. Faced with growing competition, companies must no longer simply produce at the lowest cost. They must also adapt quickly to demanding, unstable and differentiated demand.

Today, plant flexibility is facilitated by advances in automation (production processes without direct human intervention). But flexibility also concerns employees. The assembly line has not disappeared, but alongside it, particularly in large-scale industries, there are more and more manufacturing islands (responsible for sub-assemblies) entrusted to a work team. Thanks to the versatility of operators capable of occupying several positions, which requires the possession of varied skills and knowledge, we are tending to move away from the "one man, one workstation" couple to the "one team, one installation or system" couple. Noting the limits of this technical organization, some authors have advocated a humanization of work.

After the Second World War, the son of Toyota's founder, Kiichiro Toyoda, and engineer Taiichi Ono drew on the work of William Edwards Deming and Henry Ford's writings on Fordism to develop a simple but effective company management system known as the Toyota Production System (TPS), also known as Toyotism. This system takes into account the opinions of operators: they are involved in diagnosing problems and resolving them.

1.4.   Human relations theory

Australian physician Elton Mayo's (1880-1949) famous experiment at Western Electric is as follows. A group of female workers was set up: their working environment was gradually improved (breaks, working environment, etc.) and productivity increased, then returned to the starting situation and productivity continued to rise. This paradoxical result showed that the cohesion of the small group, and above all the consideration shown to these workers, were very important factors, much more so than the simple working environment.

These experiences gave rise to the School of Human Relations, which sees the workshop as a social group and the company as a social system. In particular, the group is not simply the sum of individuals at work, but an entity whose functioning can have consequences for production (good understanding, communication, etc.). The limits of Taylorism thus highlighted the importance of the human factor in business.

These new forms of organization are accompanied by the development of "participative management" aimed at involving employees more closely in the success of the production process. They are based on the construction of more or less formalized meeting groups. Called "expression groups", "progress groups" or, more often, "quality circles", these small groups of 5 to 10 volunteers from the same workshop or office meet regularly to identify, analyze and resolve the various problems encountered in day-to-day work (quality, but also safety, productivity, etc.).

1.5.   The systemic theory of the Organization

Psychosociologists Frederick Emery and, above all, Eric Trist were among the pioneers of the Tavistock Institute of Human Relations in London, set up in 1946 to study work-related problems. Eric Trist developed the idea that workgroup organization depends neither on technology nor on individual behavior, but on both; it is an open socio-technical system. Technology defines the limits of the type of organization possible, but the organization of work has social and psychological implications that are themselves dependent on technology. The study of group behavior must therefore be limited neither to the professional function of its members, nor to their psychological characteristics, since the operator's state of mind has a determining role on the state of the system. This is why they are based on the idea that the system must be organized to induce individual fulfillment and enrichment. To this end, they advocate an organization based on autonomous teams.

The Tavistock Institute of Human Relations had made it possible to link technological and social systems, which was a step forward from the classic approaches that focused essentially on organization and technology (Taylor). However, an essential aspect was still being neglected: the purpose of organizations, which, especially for companies, is essentially economic. The organization is also a socio-economic system.

From the late 1970s onwards, Henri Savail, working with Véronique Zardet at ISEOR, developed an innovative socio-economic approach at the crossroads of management science research and field action. This approach, which can also be described as "action research", is based on a representation of organizations (companies, associations, government agencies, etc.) that blurs the traditional oppositions between the economic and the social, the quantitative and the qualitative. Henri Savail justifies his approach by saying: "since management practice and academic literature have gone to great lengths to separate or even oppose: human/economic, satisfaction/profitability, productivity/quality, financial advantages/qualitative advantages, ethics/efficiency (...), the socio-economic approach aims to help companies and organizations put an end to micro-experiments in improvement, which rarely develop in a sustainable way, and never irrigate the entire company". The organization is thus seen as a complex system, resulting from the interaction between its structures (physical, technological, organizational, demographic, mental) and the behaviors of the individuals working within it (individual, group and activity, category, pressure group and collective).

Structure-behavior interaction produces both ortho-functioning, i.e. functioning in line with expectations, and dysfunctioning, i.e. non-conforming functioning. Ortho-functions fuel profitability and enable development. Dysfunctions, on the other hand, absorb energy and financial resources, and limit results.

Towards the end of the last century, a number of authors turned their attention to taking into account the legitimate interests of other company stakeholders in addition to shareholders, managers and employees, giving rise to the theory of stakeholders.

2. Stakeholder theory

Today, it is the subject of pseudo-arguments that attest to its status as a serious matter, a sign of the existence of an American intellectualism in the management sciences. The resulting proliferation of texts fills bibliographies with cross-referenced citations, and journals with texts in which both reviewers and reviewed find their accounts ... in the categories of the construction of an academic capitalism. This criticism can also be applied to this text.

The first thing to note is the speed with which the corpus has been built up, as evidenced by the proliferation of articles and conferences. The academic works of recent years have given it a privileged place. According to T. Donaldson and L. E. Preston (1995), over 100 articles and a dozen books have been devoted to the subject, the majority of them published in Business Ethics Quarterly and the Academy of Management Review. But the concept of stakeholder is still very vague. American literature often distinguishes shareholders from other stakeholders. Today, stakeholder theory tends to impose itself as a reference in discourse and through the mimicry of corporate social responsibility policies, to the point of taking on all the aspects of an ideology. Its major ambiguity also lies in the fact that non-participating parties are legitimately excluded. The question posed by this text is: why like stakeholder theory?

E. R. Freeman (1984) defines stakeholder as "any group or individual who may affect or be affected by the achievement of the company's objectives".

According to S. Mercier (1999), stakeholders are "all the agents for whom the company's development and good health are important issues".

Ethical considerations were at the origin of the development of stakeholder theory, and these considerations were used to elaborate its normative aspect (we would all be stakeholders!).

For T. Donaldson and L. E. Preston (1995), stakeholders are defined by their legitimate interest in the organization, which implies that:

□ rights holders are groups and individuals with legitimate interests; they are known and identified,

□ the interests of all stakeholder groups have intrinsic value. Today, a classic distinction is made between (A. Caroll, 1989):

□ Primary stakeholders are those with a direct, contractually determined relationship with the company (or contractual stakeholders).

☐ Secondary stakeholders, which include all those around the company who are affected by its actions, but who do not have a contractual relationship with the company (also known as diffuse stakeholders).

Other distinctions exist, such as that between internal stakeholders, classic external stakeholders and external stakeholders with power to influence, or (I. Pelle Culpin, 1998) the distinction between institutional stakeholders (those linked to laws, regulations, inter-organizational entities, industry-specific professional organizations), economic stakeholders (the players operating on the markets of the company concerned), and ethical stakeholders (emanating from ethical and political pressure organizations), which are more difficult to include.

3. CSR: consolidating the theoretical relationship between ethics and management

Conceptually, Corporate Social Responsibility is a notion whose contours are not yet well defined. At the confluence of several complementary but distinct disciplinary fields, the notion of CSR is confronted with a "conceptual vagueness" built on the idea of broadening the raison d'être of the company (Pesqueux (2009)). In this section, we present the different meanings of the concept, its measurement approaches, its theoretical determinants, as well as its supposed links with corporate financial performance.

- The different meanings of CSR

Corporate social responsibility for some (Gond & Igalens, 2012; Capron & Quairel-Lanoizelée, 2010; Turcotte & Salmon, 2007), corporate social responsibility for others (McGuire (1963), Carroll (1979), Jones (1980)), the CSR controversy already begins with the wording given to the acronym. Other similar formulations are also used to refer to the same notion. ISO (2010), for example, speaks of the societal responsibility of organizations (RSO). This latter formulation no longer confines the concept to companies alone, but extends it to any type of organization whose activities are likely to have an impact on society as a whole. Champion & Gendron (2005) use the term "corporate citizenship". Gond (2010) prefers to speak of Corporate Social Performance (CSP).

For Bowen, CSR refers to the obligations of business people to follow policies, make decisions, or follow directions that are desirable in terms of goals and values for society.

From the foundations laid by the pioneers of CSR, a number of developments have taken place. Carroll (1979), in his pyramid model, distinguishes four levels of responsibility to which the company is subject, which are not necessarily mutually exclusive: (i) economic responsibility, which consists in producing goods and services, selling them and making a profit for shareholders; (ii) legal responsibility (being legal), which involves strict compliance with the laws and regulations in force in the course of business; (iii) an ethical responsibility (to be fair), which corresponds to behaviors that are not legally required, but from which society expects a great deal from the company; (iv) a philanthropic, discretionary responsibility (to be good), which refers to everything that is left to the company's free will. The company is not economically, legally or ethically obliged to engage in this type of action, but it will have a considerable impact on its public image.

For Freeman (1984), who is seen by some as the leading figure in this theory, "stakeholder" means "an individual or group of individuals who can affect or be affected by the achievement of organizational objectives". The question remains as to which stakeholders should be taken into account, since anyone can claim an interest in a company [Sternberg, 2001; Orts & Strudler (2002); Jensen, 2002]. Another important question is how each stakeholder should be taken into account. For Palé & Ouédraogo (2016), this topic opens up yet another CSR controversy, as there is no established consensus either on which stakeholders should be retained, or on the development of criteria for assessing the level of consideration of stakeholder expectations.

CSR remains a central element of corporate ethics, on which most empirical work is based to study the relationship between ethics and performance, but it does not replace ethics.

CHAPTER IV: EMPIRICAL REVIEW OF THE INTERRELATIONSHIP BETWEEN ETHICS AND PERFORMANCE

This chapter begins by presenting the precursors of empirical studies. It then goes on to present the various studies according to the conclusions they reached, i.e. a positive relationship between ethics and performance, a negative relationship between ethics and performance, and a neutral or complex relationship between them.

1. The precursors of empirical studies

As previously mentioned, in the 1930s, the responsibility of businessmen and the moral function of corporate executives became a ubiquitous subject of analysis in managerial doctrine (Berle and Means, 1932, Bernard, 1938).

In 1975, Bowman and Haire tested the relationship between responsible behavior and corporate earnings. Based on an analysis of the annual reports of 82 companies in the food sector, they established a social responsibility score for each company. They then compared these scores with the earnings achieved by the individual companies. Their conclusion was that the relationship between profit and responsibility takes on an inverted U shape. In fact, adopting ethical behavior does not seem to imply lower profit, since the 31 companies considered to have behaved ethically all generated a higher median profit (between 12.3% and 17.1%) than the 51 with a responsibility index of 0% (i.e. a median profit of 10.2%). However, the study highlighted that beyond a certain point, profit seems to decrease. In other words, it pays to be "good", but you can't be "too good".

In 1999, Berman, Wicks, Kotha and Jones tested the relationship between financial performance and stakeholder awareness. In a first model, stakeholders were seen simply as a means of improving financial performance. In a second model, firms made a commitment to all stakeholders so that, in return for this commitment, they could benefit from a gain. But profit is not the ultimate goal, and shareholders are not given priority over other stakeholders. All groups are treated on the basis of moral commitments, and as ends in themselves in relation to these commitments.

Today, stakeholder theory is undoubtedly the most appropriate and perhaps also the most mobilizable and mobilized to model the concept of corporate social responsibility and ethics. It is a formidable management tool, both strategic and ethical.

This approach assumes that social commitment can positively influence economic performance. Based on the assumption that the most responsible companies are the best performers, social commitment becomes a reputedly profitable investment decision for companies. Numerous studies have made the connection between social responsibility and economic performance.

The results can be summarized as follows:

Positive Relationship	Negative Relationship	No Relationship
• Bragdon and Marlin (1972), • Moskowitz (1972), • Bowman and Haire (1975), • Belkoui (1976), • Heinze (1976), • Sturdivant and Ginter (1977), • Spicer (1978), • Ingram (1978), • Chen and Metcalf (1980), • Kedia and Kuntz (1981), Fry et al. (1982), • Cochran and Wood (1984), • Rockness et al (1986), • Spencer and Taylor (1987), • Cowen et al (1987), • Wokutch and Spencer (1987), • Belkaoui (1992), • Johnson and Greening (1999),	• Vance (1975), • Spicer (1978), • Kedia and Kuntz(1981), • Jarrell and Peltzman (1985), Pruitt and Peterson (1986), • Davidson et al (1987), • Davidson and Worrel (1988), • Hoffer et al (1988).	• Alexander and Buchholz (1978), • Abbott and Menson (1979), • Kedia and Kuntz (1981), • Aupperle et al (1985), • Belkaoui and Kaprik (1989), • Hackson and Milne (1996).
Positive Relationship	Negative Relationship	No Relationship
• Waddock and Graves (1997), • Griffin and Mahon (1997), • Stanwick and Stanwick (1998), • Orlitzky (2001).		

Specialized literature shows that, depending on the angle of analysis chosen, various links, sometimes contradictory, are discernible between a company's societal performance and its financial performance.

Indeed, the liberal vision, which leans towards a negative link (Friedman, 1970), is opposed by a vision postulating a positive link through the notion of social influence (Freeman, 1984[66]). Other authors postulate an absence of relationship between the two variables, and some see this relationship as a tangle of more or less complex links.

2. Studies showing a positive relationship between ethics and performance

Preston & O'Bannon (1997) are the reference works on which academic research attempting to establish the link between PES and FP is based; they constructed a typology of possible theoretical links, each type of link being a working hypothesis that researchers set out to test. Based on their ideas, numerous studies have been carried out. Allouche & Laroche (2005) and Gond (2010) provide the following summary:

> ➢ **Social Performance Positively Influences Financial Performance**

In the logic of the advocates of stakeholder theory, satisfying the needs of the company's various stakeholders ensures a good reputation for the company, which will *ultimately* lead to an increase in its financial performance (Freeman, 1984; Ulmann, 1985; Clarkson, 1995; Donaldson & Preston, 1995). The mechanism described is known as the "social impact" hypothesis of CSR (Preston & O'Bannon, 1997).

> ➢ **Financial performance has a positive impact on social performance**

This assumption, known as the "available funds hypothesis", is based on the existence of a certain financial capacity within the company, as a prerequisite for any CSR action. For Gond (2010), although companies may wish to implement socially responsible behavior, this attitude is contingent first and foremost on available resources, and the author concludes that a high level of profitability at a given moment can increase a company's ability to consolidate discretionary projects, which subsequently generates an increase in societal performance.

---

[66] Freeman, R.E. (1984) Strategic Management: A Stakeholder Approach. Pitman, Boston.

> Financial and social performance have a positive mutual influence.

This hypothesis is based on the idea of the existence of a virtuous circle. Indeed, according to Waddock & Graves (1997) and Preston & O'Bannon (1997), a high level of societal performance leads to an improvement in financial performance, which in turn offers the opportunity to reinvest in socially responsible actions. This virtuous circle can also become vicious, as poor performance in one area can worsen the situation in the other.

3. Studies showing a negative relationship between ethics and performance

> Social performance has a negative impact on financial performance

This is the assumption of liberals who are originally hostile to the notion of CSR[67]. This model postulates that taking Corporate Social Responsibility into account implies additional financial costs (e.g. investing in charity, environmental protection, community development, etc.), thereby causing a competitive disadvantage for the company (Friedman, 1962, 1970). From this perspective, any socially responsible initiative distracts managers from their goal of profit maximization (Aupperle, Carroll and Hatzfeld, 1985). The proponents of this view see CSR as an independent variable, and therefore unlikely to produce any positive induced effects. As a result, there is a trade-off to be made between better societal performance and improved financial profitability: this is the "trade-off hypothesis".

> Financial performance has a negative impact on social performance

At this level, we start from the possibility that managers may opportunistically pursue their own objectives, which may conflict with those of shareholders and other stakeholders (Williamson, 1985). Preston & O'Bannon (1997) argue that when financial performance is strong, managers will tend to increase their own profit by reducing social spending. On the other hand, if financial results are inadequate, managers will tend to redeem and justify themselves by investing more in social actions, just to have a pretext to divert shareholders' attention. This is the meaning of the "managerial opportunism" hypothesis.

---

[67] M. Foucault, 1988, Dits et Écrits, NRF, Paris, Gallimard, Tome IV.

4. Studies showing a neutral or complex relationship between ethics and performance

➢ No link between social and financial performance

Mc Williams & Siegel (2001) propose this hypothesis as a complement to that of Preston and O'Bannon (1997). To arrive at this model, the authors start from the standard microeconomic postulate of the existence of a market for social responsibility (existence of demand and supply for social responsibility). Companies therefore invest in socially responsible actions to satisfy stakeholder demand. In market equilibrium, they argue that the costs and profits generated offset each other (cancel each other out). This theoretically justifies the "neutrality hypothesis" of interactions between societal and financial performance.

➢ A more complex link between social and financial performance

For some authors (Bowman & Haire, (1975); Barnett & Salomon (2012); Moore (2001), the relationship between societal performance and corporate financial performance is complex, non-linear and in the form of an inverted "U". The implication of these authors' results is that there is an optimum level beyond which socially responsible investment no longer improves financial performance. This hypothesis alone sums up three of the above hypotheses. In fact, in the ascending part of the curve, it is the materialization of the "social impact" hypothesis, which postulates the positive effect of societal performance on financial performance; at the extreme of the curve, it is a steady-state situation where an additional level of societal performance has no effect on financial performance (the neutrality hypothesis); in the downward phase of the curve, the "trade-off hypothesis" of CSR critics is realized, insofar as any additional effort in terms of societal performance results in a drop in financial performance.

These empirical studies show that there is an interrelationship between ethics and performance in Western contexts, but that its meaning varies according to the context. We are going to check whether these conclusions can be transposed to Malian industrial companies. To begin with, we need to present the evolution of the socio-political and economic situation and managerial practices from 1960 to the present day. This overview will be the subject of the second part of this research.

CONCLUSION

In the light of recent crisis events such as the COVID 19 pandemic, it is clear that moralization has become a necessity for companies. Whether in industrialized or developing countries, there is an urgent need to consider the actions companies need to take to reduce their negative impact and increase their capacity to have a positive impact on society. As a result of globalization, the natural course of events will soon see companies thriving in developing countries take on the same societal centrality as their counterparts in developed countries. These companies will soon be "society's business", or these companies will soon be "business's business". Whether one subscribes to one or the other of these visions, it remains undeniable that companies are, for the most part, subject to an inescapable obligation, the satisfaction of which requires them to learn how to mobilize non-dependent stakeholders to a greater extent in order to achieve their economic objectives while remaining ethical. In this quest, they generally rely on the entire social body of their locality. The driving forces behind these groups of individuals are often delighted to lend a helping hand, for through their social actions and societal contributions they have become indispensable to general prosperity. As a result, ethical businesses, more than the wishful thinking of idealistic theorists, today appear to be the foundation on which tomorrow's economy in industrializing countries will rest.

It's also worth noting that, with the advent of decentralization and improved levels of education, communities, including politicians, customers and prospects, are increasingly seeking to understand the impact of companies on society, whether in terms of employment, tax payments, environmental impact, pollution or resource depletion. Consumers' heightened awareness of the challenges of sustainable development has led many partners to adopt a more responsible approach to consumption. As a result, companies are increasingly obliged to take their expectations into account.

The company must be seen as a complex body characterized by structures, behaviors and two essential functions: economic performance (producing and distributing goods and services, distributing income) and social performance, providing a suitable living environment (physical and moral) for the workforce and the community as a whole.